WILD GARDENING

STRATEGIES AND PROCEDURES USING NATIVE PLANTINGS

RICHARD L. AUSTIN

Principal Photographer: Derek Fell

A Fireside Book
Published by
Simon & Schuster, Inc.
New York

A QUARTO BOOK

Copyright © 1986 by Quarto Marketing Ltd.

A Fireside Book
Published by Simon & Schuster, Inc.
Rockefeller Center
1230 Avenue of the Americas
New York, New York 10020

FIRESIDE and colophon are registered trademarks of Simon & Schuster, Inc.

Library of Congress Cataloging in Publication Data
available upon request.

Paperback edition ISBN 0-671-60241-1   •   Hardcover edition ISBN 0-671-62022-3

WILD GARDENING: *Strategies and Procedures Using Native Plantings*
was prepared and produced by
Quarto Marketing Ltd.
15 West 26th Street
New York, New York 10010

Editor: Mary Forsell
Art Director: Richard Boddy
Designer: Mary Moriarty
Maps & Illustrations: Mary Moriarty
Photo Researcher: Susan M. Duane
Mechanicals: Michele Lerner

Typeset by BPE Graphics, Inc.
Color separations by Hong Kong Scanner Craft Company Ltd.
Printed and bound in Hong Kong by Leefung-Asco Printers Ltd.

ACKNOWLEDGMENTS

I wish to take this opportunity to express my appreciation to the Environmental Seed Producers, Inc., and the Applewood Seed Company for permission to use some of their photographs of wild-plant material. They produce native-plant-material seed mixtures for use in wild-garden compositions.

CONTENTS

THE WILD-GARDEN SYSTEMS

THE WILD-GARDEN THEMES

CONTENTS

INTRODUCTION

The Alternative Garden

When the human species began to dominate its environment, the prevailing motivation was basic survival. Having food, shelter, and protection was the essential motivation guiding most of the land-clearing and gardening practices of the past. As tribal communities expanded, the notion of personal garden plots located in close proximity to the home became more widespread. Even well into this century, people have felt the need to dominate and define their gardens and landscapes, to arrange them into more manageable habitats.

The most dominant form of landscape development in history has been that of the *formal* composition—not because of necessity but as a form of cultural expression. As people advanced in civilization, they wanted to exert increasing control over their environment. With the ornamental landscape, they created a sense of place and belonging. Amid the changing forces of the outside world, they established a secure, orderly niche through the formal garden.

As far back as ancient Egyptian times, the axis was used for structural control of the garden. By the sixth century B.C., the Greeks were developing formal courtyards and planting rows of trees around marketplaces to create public parks. And by the time of the Roman Empire, the formal garden had emerged as a space created purely for the pleasure it provides.

During the Middle Ages in Europe, many towns were fortified and developed an intricate system of walls and moats that emphasized the architectural sense of restraint. In addition, large areas of countryside were cultivated, and monasteries promoted the development of herb gardens and orchards, usually laid out in well-ordered checkerboard beds. This style began to pervade landscapes outside the monastery walls as well; the decorative garden became increasingly popular, featuring fountains, ornamental pots, and other details.

The formal garden space became the most acceptable landscape arrangement in France during the reign of Louis XIV. Intricate patterns created with clipped hedges, manicured grasses, trimmed evergreens, and ornate statuary prevailed. And because these gardens were associated with royalty and wealth, society began to equate the formal landscape with social rank and success. The royal courtyards of Persia in the early eighteenth century also exhibited a strict adherence to formalism in their layout, generally consisting of numerous, painstakingly designed small gardens.

This trend toward ornamentation with trees and shrubs continued well into the twentieth century. Such public parks as St. James Park in London and portions of Central Park in New York City continued the tradition of formal outdoor spaces. Boulevards in large cities all over the world reflected the straight lines of cathedral canopies in the even spacing of their manicured trees. Flowering shrubs and showy blossoms dominated grounds.

Backyard environments mirrored this modality with weekly-mowed lawn grasses and geometrically shaped plantings. Every vista, whether public or private, was under a structural landscape control. This was the way it had always been, and no one really questioned it—at least, not until recently.

The energy crisis of the 1970s changed more than just our technological habits. Due to the heightened awareness of our limited natural resources, automobiles have become more gas-efficient, and the modern home is being designed with an emphasis on energy-saving thermal and solar features. As our approach to living changes in these major areas, so does our concept of the modern garden. The highly structured, time-consuming landscapes of the past are less practical for our fast-paced life-styles. We now question the need for imported bulbs that require extensive cultivation, only to quickly bloom and then vanish. We are no longer sure that we want to control our landscapes to such an extent that all of our weekend time is spent keeping one Saturday ahead of the fast-growing lawn.

These issues and similar ones have guided us into a new and more exciting landscape theory—one that places the visually pleasing natural order of plant materials over that of trimmed shrubbery. It is now recognized that native plant materials offer just as much ornamental quality as conventionally used hybrids. In addition, they require less cultivation time and thrive on the natural rhythms of the outdoors. The wild garden provides a sense of liberation and a serene beauty that owes itself to natural blendings of color, form, and texture.

The home gardener is no longer considered lazy or "out of place" if prairie grasses replace manicured lawns. Native tree masses are now seen as much more practical than high-maintenance fruiting varieties. Even fallen trees and large stones have a purposeful place in the wild garden.

Just as the cycles of nature repeat themselves, so do the dogmas of civilization, and the wild garden is once again claiming its well-deserved place as a valid, aesthetically pleasing expression of nature. More than an alternative to formalism, the wild garden is our forgotten heritage. It is a simple, obtainable antidote to our fast-lane life-style—a feature that can bring us solitude and peace in a crowded world which often demands more from us than we can give. Although it is such an uncomplicated garden concept, the wild garden's rewards are far greater than its demands, for it yields a sense of tranquillity and perspective, teaching by example the natural order of priorities. It is only natural and, therefore, long overdue.

THE
WILD-GARDEN
SYSTEMS

WHEN THE WILD GARDEN
ENTERS YOUR LIFE

A small wild-flower meadow adjoins a forested overstory to provide a tranquil mix of natural plant forms. The eye is captured by ivies and mosses on the tree trunks and then led casually to a background of colorful understory.

Once you are bitten by the natural-garden bug, you will enter into a world that could be somewhat frustrating in the beginning. Numerous disappointments will thwart every effort to establish the composition. Plant materials will be difficult to locate. Neighbors will tease you (and may complain), and community officials may even cite you for growing what some people call "noxious weeds." You may run into government regulations that prevent you from collecting plants in the wild because of the Endangered Species Act. It is important to check with your local USDA Soil Conservation Service for a current species list. Native cultivation is considered impractical and undesirable by some native-plant-habitat protectionists, who may even challenge your collection of seeds from the countryside. These constraints, however, are only minor when compared to the multitudes of pleasures you will receive when your wild garden is completed. Remember also that seeds and other materials may easily be obtained through suppliers.

The beauty and serenity of the native plant species offer a special cohesiveness with the natural world not found in any other landscapes. The unstructured patterns and blending masses provide a pleasant surrounding for the enjoyment of a comfortable, relaxed life-style. Once your natural garden is established, relatively few hours will be spent "controlling" the vegetation. Less monetary resources are needed to stabilize this type of environment than that of a formal garden. These conveniences in turn create more time for you and things you like to do, while not eliminating your outdoor gardening pleasure.

Left: *A sea of wild flowers highlights this meadow-garden composition. Varieties of colorful blossoms blend gradually with small shrubs, and a mass of screening trees form a background vista.* **Below top:** *The subtle blending of early spring colors brings a smooth and restful composition to the wild garden. A sculptured bird bath and boulder outcropping are slightly hidden among the blossoms and sparkling foliage.* **Below bottom:** *Small trees and shrubs line the edge of this garden pond and overhang to provide a shaded habitat for the aquatic residents.*

BASIC PLANT SYSTEMS

The success of the wild-garden adventure is dependent upon a complex system of plant communities existing within the natural world. The trees and flowers that live and grow in New England and Nova Scotia will not repeat their performance in southern California. The tropical forests of southern Florida grow there for a reason and a purpose, as does the conifer vegetation throughout the Rocky Mountains. Each plant and group of plants has specifically evolved to inhabit a particular terrain and region. Moving them into your landscape, therefore, will require some careful thought and a general understanding of their environmental context.

When you begin to consider plant materials for your garden, you should think about how they live, where they live, and why they live where they do. The choice, location, and effective use of each plant in your garden will depend upon the external forces that affect them. These considerations should be the main factors in establishing the plant "systems" in the garden.

There are two basic plant systems to consider: the individual system and the population system. The individual system is the relationship of the plant to itself and controls how it survives and reproduces within a given environment. The population system is the relationship of one plant to another and determines how it exists within the overall plant community. These two systems acting together form the overall vegetative environments, ranging in size from a small terrarium to the entire region of the Rocky Mountains.

The ability of an individual plant to provide a specific function in the environment of your wild garden is related, in part, to its hardiness and adaptability. Hardiness and adaptability, in turn, are controlled by climate. Climate, in this sense, determines what types of plants will grow where. An individual garden plant goes through three basic stages when adapting to a climatic area: germination, vegetative growth, and flowering and fruiting. Most plants, with the exception of mosses and ferns, start from seeds. Those species that reproduce vegetatively (rhizomes, or runners) create offspring that are genetically identical to the parent plant and are called *clones*. The sources for your wild-garden materials will be primarily seeds, with a few of your larger materials coming from gathered transplants.

Climate adaptability and hardiness are controlled by temperature, water, and light. These are the same elements that affect the houseplants you may have on your porch and near a window.

An understory mass of pink dogwoods overshadows a winding pathway in this ornamental garden. The irregular spacing and nonuniform arrangement of the plants help to create the wild appearance.

The snow-covered floor of this forest garden highlights the changing seasons by contrasting dramatically with Iris reticulata, *which is pushing through the ground in a burst of spring color.*

These drought resistant Dudleya farinosa *(also known as* Echeveria farinosa) *use their gray-green leaves and their yellow-spiked flowers to shroud the boulders of this hillside landscape.*

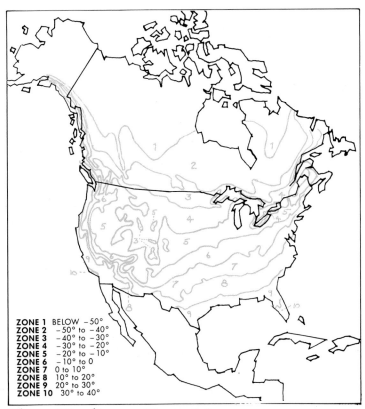

Plant Hardiness Zone Map

Gardeners use this hardiness zone map for selecting plants for their landscapes. Since it represents temperature only, however, use it along with other information to determine actual tolerance ranges. (Courtesy of the United States Department of Agriculture)

In the map legend:

ZONE 1	BELOW −50°
ZONE 2	−50° to −40°
ZONE 3	−40° to −30°
ZONE 4	−30° to −20°
ZONE 5	−20° to −10°
ZONE 6	−10° to 0
ZONE 7	0 to 10°
ZONE 8	10° to 20°
ZONE 9	20° to 30°
ZONE 10	30° to 40°

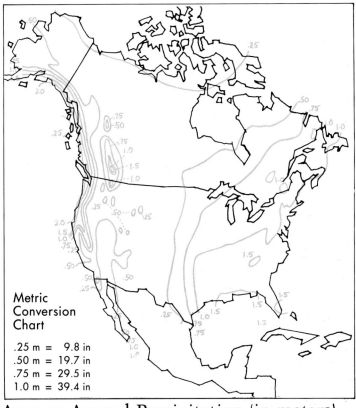

Average Annual Precipitation (in meters)

Rainfall determines a wild garden's ability to grow. Where rainfall is heavy, the climax stage could be a dense forest garden. Where it is light, a garden will be desertlike.

Metric Conversion Chart

.25 m =	9.8 in
.50 m =	19.7 in
.75 m =	29.5 in
1.0 m =	39.4 in

Temperature strongly influences plant growth. Every plant has low and high temperature extremes beyond which it cannot endure. When low readings exist for too long a period of time, the ability of the plant to reproduce itself is curtailed and the individual system dies. If readings remain too high, the environment dries out, the population systems die back, and competition expands. Some individual plants are then dominated by more aggressive species and the balanced garden becomes uncontrolled and ineffective.

Water, whether too much or too little, will also affect the way plants grow in your garden. Under water stress, an individual plant or population system will change dramatically. Without water, some plants become dormant. With too much water, they may grow too vigorously and actually crowd other species in your garden.

Light is the key element in photosynthesis and will determine the organization of plants in your wild-garden design. Exposure to sun or shade in your composition will relate to the plants' ability to reproduce effectively. You should consider these three factors:

1. The intensity of the light. Some plants actually need the shade of taller materials to prevent the loss of valuable moisture.

2. The quality of light. Light comes to earth in the form of ultraviolet and infrared rays. Some plants like more blue light (ultraviolet) while others prefer more red (infrared) light. Just because a plant receives light does not mean that it can survive under any quantity or quality of light.

3. The length of exposure to the light. Many plants in the natural environment have adapted to a "short day." Others, like many wild flowers, need a "long day" to reach their full growth potential. It is important to determine the length of the plant's "day" before it is selected and placed in your wild garden.

WHAT WILD PLANTS TOLERATE

*T*he basic plant systems and their relationships to climates are the main ingredients of what is called a plant's *tolerance range*. This range is that limit of conditions in which the plant can grow and will reproduce. A plant may be tolerant to the conditions of one area but only grow and reproduce in another. These tolerance ranges are easily identified and serve as the general guidelines for developing wild gardens. Your local native plant society can tell you what plants will work for you.

A plant is like a well-designed machine that relies on fuel resources to function. These fuel resources (light, water, temperature, and soil) are converted into elements that keep the plant "running." An interruption of the fuel supply will turn the machine off. So select your native plants carefully, bearing in mind their individual needs. When you do, the survival of the species will be ensured, and your garden will be a more tolerant environment for both the plants and you.

For a more natural effect in a tropical garden, impatiens can be used as accents along with ferns, textures of which will always add visual interest.

Wild foxglove and ferns envelop this dead tree in a natural seaside garden. In a typical ornamental landscape, the dead tree would be removed. In the wild garden, however, it is an important ingredient in the composition.

An unpaved pathway is edged by delicate blossoms as it winds its way past a large boulder.

1 North Pacific Coast
2 Willamette Valley—Puget Sound
3 Central California Valleys
4 Cascade Sierra Nevada
5 Southern California
6 Columbia River Valley
7 Palouse-Bitterroot Valley
8 Snake River Plain—Utah Valley
9 Great Basin-Intermontane
10 Southwestern Desert
11 Southern Plateau
12 Northern Rocky Mountains
13 Central Rocky Mountains
14 Southern Rocky Mountains
15 Northern Great Plains
16 Central Great Plains
17 Southern Plains
18 Northern Black Soils
19 Central Black Soils
20 Southern Black Soils
21 Northern Prairies
22 Central Prairies
23 Western Great Lakes
24 Central Great Lakes
25 Ozark-Ohio-Tennessee River Valleys
26 Northern Great Lakes—St. Lawrence
27 Appalachian
28 Piedmont
29 Upper Coastal Plain
30 Swampy Coastal Plain
31 South-Central Florida
32 Subtropical Florida

Plant Growth Regions of the United States

The United States is comprised of thirty-two general plant-growth regions, which stretch from the North Pacific Coast to the southern tip of Florida. Use these regions as a guide when planning your wild garden. (From "Landscape for Living," Washington, D.C.: USDA, 1972 p.1)

The blossoms of this prickly pear add luster to the natural form it has developed in this composition.

Seas of blooming and budding wild flowers are the emphasis in this large meadow landscape.

THE WILD FORMS OF PLANTS

Plants growing freely in their natural habitat take on a completely different growth form from that of their ornamental cousins. Nature has designed a beautiful and unique relationship for plants in the wild. To move them into a garden environment requires a duplication of this natural form.

Conifers, for instance, are most often used in an ornamental setting as screens or accent elements. The homeowner often trims up or prunes them into desired shapes to enhance a garden's overall design. In the wild habitat, the natural shape is always undisturbed unless interrupted by overcrowding, storm damage, or insect infestation. Pruning, however, occurs naturally. As the conifer grows to maturity, the lower portion of the branches tends to "die off," leaving an often messy appearance. In the wild garden, these lower branches should remain undisturbed. As they fall to the ground and decay, they provide needed compost for the associated plants growing beneath the tree.

The natural shape and form of a plant should dominate the wild garden. Each individual plant must relate to others of the same species and to the overall masses of the total composition. Natural forms as they occur in wild habitats, called *life forms*, are important if the final survival of the materials is to be ensured.

The largest of the life forms is the *overstory tree*. In the ornamental garden, they are called *shade trees*. The overstory may reach a height of two-hundred feet or more (although that height will be difficult to achieve unless the tree is already existing naturally on the site). Large oaks and California redwoods are prime examples of overstory trees.

The overstory is followed in height by

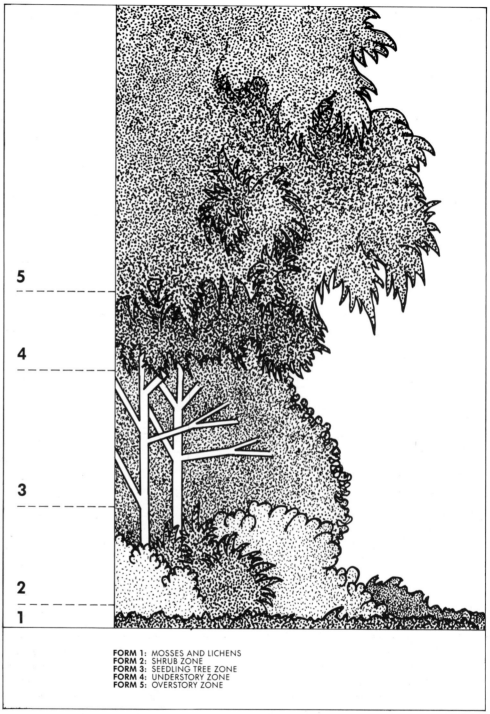

FORM 1: MOSSES AND LICHENS
FORM 2: SHRUB ZONE
FORM 3: SEEDLING TREE ZONE
FORM 4: UNDERSTORY ZONE
FORM 5: OVERSTORY ZONE

The wild forms of plants that will comprise the structures of the natural-landscape garden consist of mosses and lichens, shrubs and herbs, seedling trees, understory trees, and overstory (canopy) trees.

A natural, restful nook is created with this informal arrangement of plant massings.

Large rhododendrons act as understory blooms for this forest garden. Small wood ferns and fallen leaves provide the groundcover.

A wooded hillside slopes into a slow-moving stream lined with dazzling shrubs and wood ferns.

the *understory tree*. This form depends on the shade of the overstory to survive. It requires this protection to fulfill its basic needs. A dogwood blooming in spring underneath the shaded forest is a good example of an understory. The more ornamental dogwood varieties have been developed to reduce the dependence upon an overstory. That is why you often see them standing alone in a sunlit garden.

Next comes the *seedling tree*. It, too, needs the protection from both understories and overstories to germinate from a seed and begin vegetative growth. Some of these species, in ten to twenty years, surpass their more mature protectors and eventually become part of the overstory.

Following the seedling tree, we find the *shrubs and herbs*. These forms are most often used in gardens because they are readily available and easy to handle. They are also the major source of food for

many types of wildlife because of their low-growing form.

At the lower end of the forms chain, we find *mosses and lichen*. These are the natural groundcovers of the environmental garden and often grow upon large roots and fallen trees. Although it is sometimes difficult to locate individual plants for your needs, a rock, boulder, or stump already covered with these plants can be readily moved into your compositon.

WHERE WILD PLANTS LIVE

The mixture of meadow plants with a backdrop of forest trees provides a rich treat for the eyes.

When you begin to consider what plants are feasible for your wild garden, you will soon discover that plants live in unexpected places. Some, like the common cattail, will only grow near lakes or ponds. Willows and cottonwood always live near water (their presence in a meadow indicates a high water table). Mesquite trees, on the other hand, like very dry sites. Their root systems dig deep into the soil to locate water. To use these materials in a wild-garden compositon, the habitat you create for them must be very similar to their native environment.

Plants live where they do because they can "tolerate" the environment around them. To thrive in a cold winter, as do pines and firs, their leaves may have developed into needles to reduce the vulnerable surface area. Or, if they are deciduous, they will shed their leaves during extended periods of cold. If the climate is hot, humid, and wet from excessive rainfall, the leaves may be large and broad to hasten moisture evaporation. Mountaintop vegetation has adapted to the continuous cold weather simply by adjusting its growth needs to a shortened growing season and rapid reproductive cycle.

Adaptation to environmental conditions is also evident in plants that grow near the seashore. The air and water surrounding these plants has a high salt content, so salt-tolerant species predominante in these areas. Since these plants have become dependent upon the salt, transplanting them to an inland area will cause them to wither and die.

When you take into account the factors of climate, tolerance range, and natural geographic habitat, you begin to see a unique pattern developing. Scientists refer to this pattern as *successional growth*, in which plants develop and grow in a specific, predictable sequence.

There are two types of successional sequences. The first is *primary succession*, which begins where there is no soil base. Rock outcroppings from exposed erosions and volcanic lava are examples. Under natural geological conditions, the first plants to appear are lichens. As the rock crevices become filled with soil (normally in fifty to one-hundred years), small herbs and mosses will appear. In about one-thousand years, a tree canopy develops and stabilizes the environment.

Obviously, you cannot wait so long for your tree cover, but you can duplicate this successional stage in your garden. Stones and large boulders should be arranged in outcroppings. Partial coverage by soils or fine gravel will accelerate the emergence of small herbs and tiny shrubs. Existing trees should line the garden edges, and small masses or wild flowers should accent the sunny spots.

The second type of succession is called *secondary succession* and occurs where a soil base is present but the plants have been removed (for example, as a result of a severe fire or manmade clearing). Within the first five years following devegetation, annual plants and flowers will establish themselves. Gradually, perennial grasses, small shrubs, and young pine trees take hold. These new materials will occupy the site for another fifteen years.

Large pine trees dominate for another twenty-five years or so, until the hardwood species begin to grow. Finally, after about two-hundred years, the habitat reaches what is called the *climax stage* of growth. Although two-hundred years of growth cannot be compressed into your backyard landscape, you can select a portion of the sequence for a wild garden.

Annual herbs and small wild flowers can be chosen for a presentation at first. Then, after several years, shrubs and seedling trees can be added. With enough space, it is possible to progress from wild flowers to tall canopy trees, allowing a "minisuccession" to be displayed.

A prairie coneflower stands out among a sea of stones and tiny sedums.

Sea pinks mass along this hillside composition to protect the soil and stabilize the landscape. Not only do they serve a function, but also they help create a stunning view.

Delicate mosses and massings of ferns cover the ground of the forest composition. A small pool adds glassy highlights to the floor and attracts birds and small mammals to the space.

The Life Forms of Plants as They Occur in Their Natural Habitat

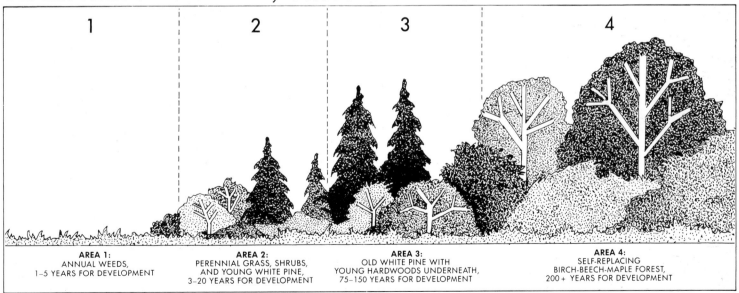

AREA 1:
ANNUAL WEEDS,
1–5 YEARS FOR DEVELOPMENT

AREA 2:
PERENNIAL GRASS, SHRUBS,
AND YOUNG WHITE PINE,
3–20 YEARS FOR DEVELOPMENT

AREA 3:
OLD WHITE PINE WITH
YOUNG HARDWOODS UNDERNEATH,
75–150 YEARS FOR DEVELOPMENT

AREA 4:
SELF-REPLACING
BIRCH-BEECH-MAPLE FOREST,
200 + YEARS FOR DEVELOPMENT

Secondary succession is the natural habitat most easily duplicated in the wild garden. It consists of annual plants, perennial grasses, shrubs and young pine trees, older pines and small hardwoods, and climax pine and hardwood materials.

THE WILD-GARDEN THEMES

WHY SELECT A THEME?

All landscape compositions have a theme. Whether they are natural environments developed over eons of time or manmade environments created on a busy Saturday morning, specific planting arrangements have been made, either by nature or by the gardener. Nature uses the elements of the environment to carefully locate plant materials. From rolling hills with forest edges to majestic oaks near a riverbank, the theme is maintained. The homeowner, too, should enhance a theme or central focus when adding rose masses or an espalier to his front lawn.

The components of the midcontinent tall-grass prairie system are placed methodically by nature with specific intent. The salt marshes of coastal grasslands also have a reason for their placement.

Conifer and hardwood forests throughout the regions are naturally mixed in order to provide optimum growing conditions for both kinds of trees.

The wild garden must be approached in its design and development with the same detail as the more formal landscapes of cut flowers and clipped hedges. To challenge and distort the natural laws of native plant communities would invite disorganization and failure. Following a theme will ensure an adherence to the values that establish original plant systems, and the wild garden will thrive for your personal enjoyment.

The premise for any wild garden should be developed from the concepts of successional growth, geographic distribution, and species tolerance factors. Bearing

Top: Flowering dogwoods are a natural understory for a forest composition. Their early spring blossoms herald the appearance of warmer days for the wild garden. **Bottom:** *A grassy clump next to a garden pond brings the meadow to the water in this wild composition.* **Right:** *A variety of plant-material masses blend together to impart a breathtaking beauty to this meadow composition.*

Left: Variegated primulas accent this water feature to bring color and excitement to a natural space. **Below top:** *An unpaved pathway passes through bright clusters of flowers as it leads into a dense forest garden.* **Below bottom:** *In a soft-palette arrangement, this seaside meadow is covered with masses of yellow and white blossoms.*

these concepts in mind, a homeowner will discover that plant selection and exterior spatial organization will be made easier and the final composition will be more attractive.

Essentially, there are three predominant types of wild-garden compositions: the *woodland garden*, the *meadow garden*, and the *water garden*. Each has unique features that make it a desirable garden environment. However, each theme also has various levels of complexity that demand careful attention.

The woodland garden, for instance, is dominated by overstory canopies and understory species that often completely cover the garden space. Very little sunlight, if any, reaches into the garden. If you want bright plant colors in your space, this theme may not be a satisfying one for you.

The meadow garden, on the other hand, needs lots of sunlight for long periods of the day. Most of its plants will not survive in large areas of shade from canopy materials. Even shadows cast from adjacent buildings will interrupt the light needed for grasses and shrubs.

The water garden may attract unwanted pests into the home. (However, it may also attract breathtaking forms of wildlife.) In many communities, this garden theme may even be against local ordinances because of potential health problems; but when executed properly, it will lend a shimmery brilliance to your landscape.

Each theme has its specific problems and advantages for the home garden. Choosing the right theme will depend on the specific benefits your region offers.

THE WOODLAND GARDEN

Tiny forget-me-nots cover this delicate aesthetic area of a forest composition.

The woodland or forest theme is probably the most popular. People seem to associate garden beauty with trees. Without an overhead planting, some feel, there is no garden. This preference is seen in the continuous overuse of trees in the formal landscape. For those individuals who like trees, the woodland garden is the answer. When combined with small clearings and open meadow areas, it provides an attractive and comfortable living environment.

The Natural Ingredients

The climate of the woodland garden consists of the amount of light reaching the treetops, the air temperatures, moisture levels, and storm activities. Although sunlight is critical to the survival of most plants, it will not be a serious problem in this wild garden. Moisture can be added during dry periods, and storm frequencies are fairly predictable.

Sunlight will reach the majority of the canopy unless obstructed by larger buildings. Each plant within the overstory has its own particular needs with regard to adapting to available light. For instance, the overstory trees usually have larger leaves because more energy is needed to conduct photosynthesis. A large canopy tree needs more food than a small one, and the larger leaves fulfill that need. The understory material, on the other hand, does not require such large leaves. If its leaves were too large, it would grow too fast for its habitat. Therefore, to provide the proper amount of light to the tree canopies in your wild garden, select the wide-structure leaves for the taller overstory and the more narrow-structure leaves for the adjacent understory.

Air temperature is also important for the forest themes. Trees need oxygen for survival just as people do. As above-ground temperatures fluctuate, air moves around to replenish the oxygen supply near the surface of the leaves. Since the trees breathe through tiny holes in the surface of their leaves, it is important not to obstruct air movement through your garden. Allow air "corridors" in your composition to prevent hot-air pockets and stagnation. If the plants dry out from lack of oxygen, the dependency habitat from plant to plant will be destroyed.

Rainfall, relative humidity, and fog are important components of the moisture requirements in a woodland garden. Some tree species require more humidity than others, so their use in a dry urban or suburban climate would not be feasible. Low-lying valleys are good locations for these humidity lovers because the movement of moisture helps these plants retain vital fluids.

Although you can't control the rainfall within your region, the introduction of irrigation systems will help the woodland landscape during times of drought. Be sure, however, that all parts of the plant are watered. The crown of the trees, the limbs, the bark, and the roots should all receive moisture.

If you live in areas where violent spring storms are frequent or where ice and snow damage is an annual occurrence, pay careful attention to the placement of your tree garden. Fast-growing tree species are very easily damaged by these acts of (continued on page 30)

Moss-covered trees and large wood ferns line a partially secluded pathway that leads into a densely planted forest garden.

This appealing woodland garden setting reflects nature's ability to sustain varied forms of life within one environment.

The Forests of North America

The basic structure of the woodland garden should reflect the specific characteristics of the planting region in which the garden is located. In addition to the thirty-two general growth areas within the United States, there are six types of forest areas. These plant communities should act as the guide for establishing your garden format. Although large trees are the main elements, the composition of related materials is also important.

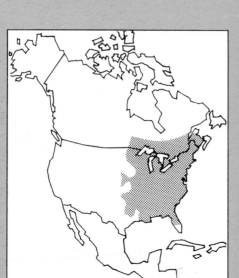

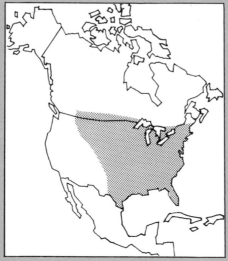

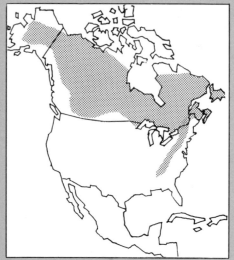

The North American Deciduous Forest

A tall canopy layer reaching one-hundred feet in height characterizes this forest environment. The understory is made up of suppressed individuals of the same overstory species. Shrubs and herbs are abundant.

The Floodplain Forest

In this forest, tall- and medium-height trees mix with small meadows and open areas of grass. Clusters of seedling trees and shrubs are common and blend into grassy plantings.

The Boreal Coniferous Forest

These materials are primarily evergreen, with few hardwoods suitable for the home garden. Pines with long needles, and spruce and fir with short needles are typical. The climate is always cool, with a large amount of annual precipitation.

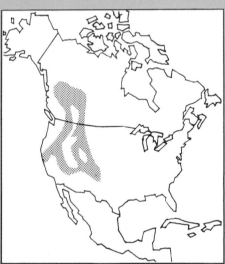

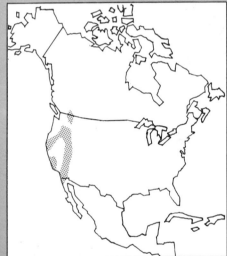

The Montane Coniferous Forest and Alpine Communities

This forest consists mostly of pines and firs with alpine meadows dispersed below. There are hardwoods at the lower and middle elevations, while pines grow on the higher slopes. Alpine meadows make up the lowest areas.

The Northern Pacific Coast–Rainy Western Hemlock Forest

A tall, thick vegetation canopy dominates this forest. Heights may reach more than two hundred feet. Understory materials have a difficult time surviving unless openings are provided in the overstory. Shrubs and smaller materials are almost nonexistent. This wild garden consists primarily of very large trees.

The Broad Sclerophyll– Grizzly Bear Community

The plants in this community are a mixture of trees and grasses. Large canopies make an overhead for small shrubs and grasses. Some areas of the southernmost portion of this forest are actually undergrowth masses with scattered trees.

nature. If you place them too close to your house or too near activity areas, damage to you or your home may occur. If overstory material is damaged by rainstorms or snows, they may in turn damage understory material and smaller plants.

The topography of your site is also critical if you are to achieve your goals in the wild garden. The most important issue is the orientation of the slopes. Do the trees you want require a north, south, east, or west orientation? If a west-facing slope is important, then a northern orientation of the plants will rob them of needed sunlight. A tree living on a natural north slope would not survive if planted on the heated exposure of a western slope.

Soil qualities of the woodland theme will influence the success or failure of your composition. A soil that is too acid or too basic will interrrupt the breakdown of nutrients for the plant. Just make sure the soil conditions on your site are compatible with the plant growth region in your area.

For instance, a pine forest will usually have a thick matting of decomposed pine needles covering the ground. These materials have accumulated over time and provide necessary high-acid nutrients for the trees. A deciduous forest is very similar to the pine woodland. Its matting consists of several types of leaves but is less acid. Remember the following hints when establishing your woodland garden soil base:

1. If decomposed matter is not already present, simply add decomposing leaves or tree bark to the top several inches of soil. This will allow the plant food nutrients to immediately benefit the trees.

2. If decomposed matter is present, allow fallen leaves or needles to remain on the ground. They will continue to decompose naturally and provide the needed foods for your trees.

The best method of determining the status of decomposed matter is to examine it to a depth of about three feet. If the soil base at this depth is dark in color, is loose when pressed, and has sand particles or rotted sticks mixed in, then the base is adequate for a wild garden. If these ele-

ments are not present, you may have to add them.

High water tables or poorly drained soils that hold water may actually drown some plant species. Some soils have more rock particles than others, and will drain water too quickly, while some may contain a high quantity of decomposed matter and will retain more water. Although the condition of your garden's soil can be modified in most situations, it is important to understand the plants' requirements before you begin.

You must consider, for instance, the seasonal aspects of the woodland garden. The most active times will be the spring and summer months, but the fall and winter variations should not be overlooked.

In the early spring, flowering seedling trees will add color and fragrance to the atmosphere. Combine them with accents of small flowering shrubs and forest wild flowers, and soon the composition creates excitement and activity. Within the canopy area, you can use flowering vines to extend colors high into the overhead zone. This usage helps to attract wildlife that may be too afraid to approach blossoms near the ground.

The bright colors of spring soon pass into the crispness of summer and monochromatic greens. Their softness quiets even the most pressured spirits. Edging masses of summer wild flowers can fill the open spaces washed with sunlight. Wild flowers will attract lovely butterflies with decorative qualities that add an enchanted touch to the garden.

Not only the verdant greens of summer, but also the sharp reds and yellows of the

Top: *This California landscape is highlighted by blended masses of small shrubs that beautifully introduce a woodland theme.* **Center:** *Ornamental* Ajuga reptans *takes on a more wild-growing appearance by mixing with the native annuals.* **Bottom:** *The authentic woodland garden should reflect the whims of nature. Here, a fallen tree settles naturally into the groundcover masses.*

fall should be planned with serious dedication. Masses of changing colors are exciting, and their appearance both close up and at a distance is an important aspect of the composition. Trees with intricate bark patterns can also act as compositional elements and emerge into the sunlight as leaves begin to cover the ground. Even the floor of matted leaves plays a part in the design and control of the overall environment.

When winter comes and the snows fall, many people forget the out-of-doors and the garden areas. The wild garden, however, is waiting for attention. Without its cover of leaves, the majesty of the canopy structure unfolds. When a blanket of soft winter snow is added, your woodland garden becomes a glistening, elegant addition to the landscape.

The Planting Structure

The planting structure of the woodland garden can take on a variety of finished forms. Often, woodland gardens are developed in a preexisting forest; however, it is quite possible to shape an open setting into a woodland garden by integrating shade-giving trees with forest shrubs and flowers. It is not necessary to use all five life forms of wild plants to achieve success. For instance, if you have a predominant overstory already existing on the site, you may wish to add only a few understory trees. Supply the composition with a fern mass or two, sprinkle a small shrub mass here and there, and you have your garden. Its central focus is the major canopy elements, with support from the understory forms.

Do not assume that since wild flowers seem to grow just about anywhere that they can easily be adapted into your wild garden without a little prior consideration. For instance, the shade of evergreens may be too much for certain wild flowers and shrubs, or there may already be a ground-cover of dense native plants that will not allow the introduction of others. If you wish to use more understory trees, seedling trees, and shrub masses, you can create "pockets" of open areas for sunlight and wild flowers. For seclusion and heavy screening, thick masses of understory and seedling trees will block undesirable views.

Large boulders and vine-covered canopies bring a natural accent to this ornamental landscape.

The twisted branches of this understory impart elegance and a sense of life to the composition even when flowers are not in bloom.

THE MEADOW GARDEN

Wild flowers and attractive annuals create a serene view across an alpine meadow composition.

This restful composition is just the opposite of the forest garden. While the wooded landscape encloses with thick overhead canopies and dense edge materials, the meadow opens up to expose surrounding vistas. With the visual impediments removed, a gardener can view faraway horizons, and rising and setting suns can spread their aura across the composition. This garden's open-air feeling and bright, sunny personality will make one's spirit feel unbounded and excited. If openness is your desire, then you should consider the meadow theme.

The Natural Ingredients

The climate of your meadow landscape will be determined more by its geographic location than by any other factor. The mountain ranges of North America block a large amount of the moisture that moves across the continent from the west. This blockage creates a drier, more arid climate on the downwind (alee) side of the ranges. This lack of moisture creates, in turn, a favorable climate for grasslike plants.

Sunlight and air movement play an important role in this composition. Many of the plants you select for your meadow will require extended periods of daylight to achieve their maximum growing capabilities. Massive shadows from trees or adjacent structures will restrict the development of the space. Without large amounts of sunlight, the meadow plantings will not be able to flower and reproduce properly.

(continued on page 36)

The North American Grasslands

North America is comprised of eight major grassland regions, whose composition can guide you in establishing your meadow garden. These areas illustrate specific grass and small-shrub groupings that can be a source for design elements as well as for the plants you will need.

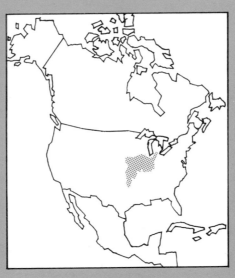

Eastern Prairie Edge

This grassland region is a transitional zone between the central plains and the deciduous forests of the eastern continental areas. Occupying vast areas from upper Ohio into Kansas and Oklahoma, it is comprised primarily of natural open meadows with sparsely mixed shrub clumps. Small to large tree masses do occur but only along water sources, such as streams, lakes, and rivers.

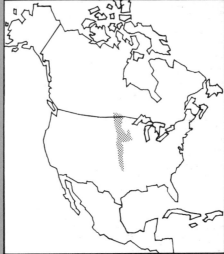

Tall-Grass Prairie

Extending from Oklahoma northward into Minnesota and Canada, this region is the most characteristic of a meadow landscape. Its bright profusion of picturesque wild flowers has been the subject of many professional and amateur photographers. Some of its grass species reach three feet in height and are found in large masses. Where the terrain is rolling, the trees grow only in the low, protected niches.

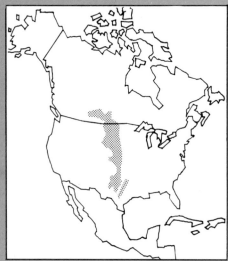

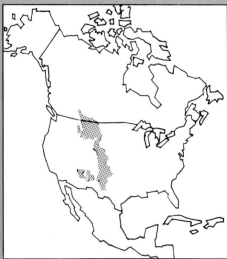

Coastal Prairie

This lowland region is found primarily in Texas and Louisiana, and is characterized by salt-tolerant grasses and periods of heavy rainfall and high humidity. On the coastline, tidal fluctuations limit the number of plant species viable for a garden. Where trees occur, they are usually fragile and susceptible to frequent storm damage during the spring and summer months.

Mixed-Grass Prairie

Moving westward from the tall-grass areas and extending northward to southern Saskatchewan, the grassland region shows a mixture of both tall- and short-grass masses, neither of which is too dominant. Shrubs are small and occur in large clumps. Trees are located in protected areas below the exposed tops of the rolling hills.

Short-Grass Prairie

As one approaches the Rocky Mountains from the east, the effects of moisture restrictions from the alee slopes become increasingly apparent. The decrease in moisture restricts the plants' growth and limits their size. Shrubs of any noticeable height are absent unless one looks near natural sources of water. Tree masses are scarce but do occur near water channels or lakes.

Bunch-Grass Desert Shrub

This prairie landscape is subject to very harsh environmental conditions. Long periods of heat and drought place extreme hardships on garden areas. Very few trees can survive this area, but some may occur in small numbers and limited size. Moisture, in the form of infrequent and violent rainstorms, drains quickly into the sands. Plants in this area undergo continued periods of dormancy from frequent droughts.

Sagebrush Grassland

Nestled among the open areas of the Rocky Mountains is the sagebrush meadow landscape. Grasses are prevalent and small shrubs (sages) dominate. Moisture is usually high because it is trapped by the mountain range. Rolling valleys of this grassy landscape blend into masses of forest areas, where snows accumulate annually.

California Grassland

This landscape located within California has an abundance of wild flowers that provide excellent accents for the garden. Drought-tolerant grasses mix with showy flowers in numerous varieties of plant combinations. Trees in the more desertlike areas are very limited, and the height of most native plants is limited to a few feet. Shrubs are sparse and grow more as individuals than in masses.

Sunlight should reach the majority of the garden area for most of the daylight hours. Limited, early-morning shadows will not deter plant growth unless these shadows persist for several hours.

Air movement, too, is important. During times when rainfall is heavy, the grasses and small shrubs in your composition must be able to dry quickly. Stem damage and diseases are a threat if excess moisture does not evaporate. Airborne pollen must be allowed to move freely through the space if the blossoms are to achieve their showy best.

Rainfall within the meadow landscapes will vary, again depending upon geography. On the southeastern edge of the major prairie areas from Oklahoma to Illinois, the amount can reach forty inches annually. In upper North Dakota, and into Alberta and Saskatchewan, the amount might not exceed twenty inches. Because of the highly variable climates within these landscapes, the predominant plants are sturdy species of grasses and small shrubs. These types of materials are hardy enough to withstand low rainfall amounts in winter and extended periods of drought in the summer. This climate-adaptability factor will be the major guide for you when you select plants for your garden.

The topography of the meadow garden is more gradual and usually less severe than that of a forest area. Strong trees often push their roots deep into the soil on steeper slopes. This prevents erosion from uprooting the plants. Weaker grasses, however, are more likely to be damaged by the movement of soils or water.

Soils for the meadow garden are easy to provide. They are usually very rich in humus and dark in color. They have good texture and a high moisture quality. With soil amendments readily available at local nurseries and garden centers, the building

Top: A chromatic mixture of blossoms is the principal focus of this meadow theme. Bottom: Lilies and purple iris blossoms are colorful additions to the grasses of this prairie composition.

of an adequate soil base for your meadow should not be difficult. The first step would be to collect a sample from a nearby natural meadow and have it analyzed by a soil specialist also known as an *agronomist*. After the soil structure has been determined, simply plan the necessary additives to achieve the required growing base.

The seasons of the meadow theme will pass in regular order, with noticeable changes in colors and textures. While large shade trees show their bright fall colors with sudden profusion, the grasses of the meadow change in a more gradual fashion.

During the cold winter months, your meadow will probably have a covering of snow. As it drifts endlessly from the prevailing winds, the crystal cover will eventually make way for the early spring blossoms and warm season grasses. Some may even appear before the final melting of snow, creating interesting textures and patterns. As the entire composition begins to take on a hue of April green, the seedlings of midsummer grasses will arise and add their crispness to the scene.

By the time summer is well under way, a kaleidoscope of bright colors will dominate the meadow. Wild flowers will be at their peak, and even some species of grasses may expose their often inconspicuous flowers.

As this beautiful time slowly edges its way into fall, the taller forbs and small shrubs begin to show themselves. No longer hidden by the myriad of summer colors, these meadow inhabitants begin to display their colorful golds and deep yellows. Even their stems and leaves add splashes of subtle accents.

The Planting Structure

The best way to describe the meadow garden is to name it an "ocean of grasses." Unlike other gardens, this landscape will have very few plants above three to four feet in height. Although it can include a great variety of colors and low-growing forms, virtually the only plants to be used are small shrubs, grasses, and seasonally active wild flowers. Clumps of larger shrubs and seedling trees may be planted on the northern- and southernmost edges of the garden for limited screening purposes, but they must not restrict sunlight upon the space during critical spring and summer periods.

A wild-flower meadow is a lovely focal point in the valley below.

Black-eyed Susans dominate this meadow garden with washes of bright yellow.

Perennial gaillardia offers a subtle color wash for this meadow.

THE WATER GARDEN

The alternative to a garden based on a forest or meadow theme is the water garden. As an independent element or as a specific feature combined with the other themes, the water garden is a popular landscape component. It can be represented as a large pond encompassing an entire garden site. It can be a small, reflecting pool at the edge of a hill, used to mirror the colors of adjacent wild flowers and trees. Or it can be a fresh, flowing stream passing lazily under the branches of a forest canopy. With a little creativity, this garden feature will attract rare species of birds and small animals to your outdoor space.

If your garden already has naturally wet soil, why not simply surrender to the wisdom of nature and create a water garden, rather than trying to alter the character of the landscape with the addition of sand or drainage pipes? If one part of your garden is lower than the rest, this would make a particularly favorable pond site. Or if your soil is very acid and the habitat is wet, you might consider allowing a natural bog to form. There are numerous possibilities, but before you can choose the right water feature for your garden, you must acquaint yourself with particular features of this environment.

The Natural Ingredients

As with the other wild-garden themes, the climate of the water garden is controlled by the geography of the site. Dry climates may require a mechanical source for this type of landscape. Wet climates may require more maintenance to slow the growth of the selected plants. In many cases, the best approach may be to use the theme in combination with either the forest or the meadow garden, to add that special touch needed to make your home landscape truly unique.

Topography will be one of the more important factors in your garden. If you want to collect water for a pond or pool, there must be a depression on the site. It must be large enough to contain your garden features and have edges that are relatively stable.

If you desire a running-water feature, there must be enough slope to allow it to flow downhill across the site. If the grade is too gradual, pooling may occur. If the grade is too steep, uncontrolled erosion may damage the site.

Regardless of the topography, the gardener must have complete control of the water at all times. It must be moved and directed to locations best suited for the plants. Uncontrolled water will disrupt the balance between plant materials and destroy the overall appearance of the landscape.

The level of the water feature is also very important. Frequently fluctuating levels will create disorder within the plant communities and may ruin the effect you wish to create in your garden. If water levels change over time, they must change slowly and relate to the seasonal changes as well as the natural needs of the plants. If you choose this feature for your garden, you can manage the level of a pond or pool with the help of these guidelines:

1. Lowering the water level may permit the germination of plants occurring naturally along the edge. It may also permit the soil to dry for short periods and allow cracking of the bottom, which allows new seeds to germinate in the garden.

2. Raising the water level may remove some undesirable plants when other maintenance methods are inefficient. It may also allow the development of deep

This water feature is perfected by natural masses of lush aquatic plants.

A slow-moving stream across a rock outcropping is a beautiful addition to any natural landscape.

A small, rocky pool is a charming focal point in this forest garden.

This water theme is heavily massed with both deep and floating aquatic plants. Weeping willow and bamboo screens ensure privacy.

aquatic plants, which bring oxygen to the water, allowing fish to thrive and give back carbon dioxide to the plants.

If both plants and animals are to make your water garden their home, the chemistry and the suspended nutrients of the water must be carefully monitored. Heavily acidic waters will require one type of plant base, and alkaline waters another. An excessive amount of either nitrogen or phosphorus will alter the chemical makeup of the system and increase free-floating algae.

Still-water features require a soil base capable of holding the water over time to maintain a constant level. What drainage occurs must be very slow. If it is too rapid, the body of water must be "fed" a fresh supply of water periodically.

Flowing water requires a very stable base in order to prevent erosion. Plant materials and essential nutrient sources will be destroyed if water moves too freely through your garden.

The Planting Structure

There are three types of water-garden structures suitable for the residential landscape: the *spring*, the *pond*, and the *small lake*.

The spring is usually a natural or artificial feature with no visible source of water. It may "bubble-up" from a soil base or run briskly out from between an arrangement of stones. Near this element you can plant small herbs like the water poppy or larger shrubs like the basket willow. It is primarily a small feature, not more than a few feet in diameter from edge to edge. It's inconspicuous in appearance and is often used as a source of water for wildlife.

The pond is much more extensive a structure than the spring but is rarely larger than twenty-five feet in diameter. It has a

Rainfall Areas for Water Gardening

Water gardens are practical in almost any climate condition. Even in the cold northern areas where winters are harsh and the snowfall is plentiful, a water garden can be an exciting alternative. It is best, however, to base your decision upon the amount of rainfall your area will receive during an average year. Both temperature and humidity are important, but these factors have a tendency to fluctuate more than the rainfall amounts. Besides, if there is a shortage of natural water, you

Areas of 5 to 25 Inches Per Year

If you live within one of these areas, you may have a difficult time maintaining a stable water level or flow in any type of water feature. The availability of natural water is not sufficient to support aquatic plants without excessive amounts of supplementary water. A water garden in these areas is not recommended unless you wish to add a sump pump to maintain the waterline.

Areas of 26 to 50 Inches Per Year

A spring or pond water feature may do very well in these areas if a supplementary water supply is available for occasional support. Loss of water from evaporation will be the most critical problem.

can temporarily add water from an artificial source until a more natural supply is available. If you want to build this feature into your wild landscape, it is important to base your decision upon the characteristics of the following rainfall areas:

Areas of 51 to 60 Inches Per Year

These rainfall areas will support springs, ponds, and small lakes. The small lake, especially, will be an attractive addition to your composition if you live within this rainfall zone. Many aquatic plants are available for your use and wildlife is plentiful for most of the seasons.

visible source of water which is often a small waterfall. Larger plants like the cattail grow near its edge, and it's also a suitable habitat for floating duckweed. The depth of the water should reach approximately three or four feet at the deepest point. Water lilies add sparkling accents to the wild composition and require a depth of at least two feet.

The small lake is the most dominant of the water-garden structures. It ranges in size from about fifty feet across to as much as one-hundred feet. All of the major aquatic plants can be grown in this feature, especially the large royal water lily. Fish and water fowl will thrive here during most seasons of the year. Its source of water is a flowing stream or channel creating an inlet or cove.

The planting masses most common to the woodland and meadow themes are not always present in the water garden. Plants near a water feature are there *because* of the water, which supplies the extra amount of moisture and nutrients needed for their survival. Different plant groups have different relationships to the water source, as follows:

1. *Perimeter plantings* are the plants that grow near the outer edge of the water garden. The root systems of these materials are adapted to high water tables. They can survive quite well in saturated soils. Such plants may include grasses, small shrubs and seedling trees, and canopy materials adapted to high water levels.

2. *Marginal aquatics* are plants that grow with their root systems in shallow water and have their crown above the waterline. They usually consist of the stronger varieties of grasses, small shrubs and seedling trees.

3. *Floating aquatics* are plants that live on the surface of the water. Their roots are suspended below the surface and their crown above the surface. They help deflect sunlight and prevent the buildup of algae in the water.

4. *Deep aquatics* are the plants that require a water depth of ten inches or more

A meandering stream brings valuable moisture to a groundcover of moss and small ferns.

to thrive. Their roots are planted in the soil base at the bottom of the pond or stream. They are very important for the production of oxygen in the feature.

When planting perimeter, marginal, or deep aquatics specimens in your water garden, make sure that the holes you've dug are deep enough for the roots to really take hold. Make sure also that the newly planted specimens are saturated with water in the first few critical weeks. If you are transplanting, choose a cool day in a moist, rainfall period; use a container that will hold water so the plants can be submerged when they are moved. You may find that over time, those plants that you have so carefully planted in a particular location have rearranged themselves in relation to other plants. This is only nature doing its own designing, and balancing the habitat to the best advantage.

ORGANIZING YOUR GARDEN

Small rocks and stepping stones create accessible areas where people may walk without endangering the delicate plant materials.

THE FUNCTIONAL AREAS

It is important to consider the spatial layout of your landscape design before you actually select the plants for your garden. Within most compositions there should be *activity areas* to meet your functional needs; *utility, or service, areas* to meet your supportive needs; and *aesthetic areas* to meet your personal needs. Each area has a specific purpose within the garden and must be carefully organized to protect the sensitive communities of wild plants.

Activity areas are those spaces where human contact with plants may be extensive or even continuous. Patios, outdoor cooking areas, and children's play areas are just a few examples. Native plants chosen for these locations should be very hardy and able to withstand constant human intrusion. Grasses selected for these areas must be sturdy and able to recover quickly after damage. Small shrubs are in danger of being crushed or partially broken. These materials, too, must be strong and able to add new growth soon after breaking. Trees are the least threatened but should have strong bark characteristics and a high natural branching height.

Utility areas are spaces where there is some human intrusion, but less than in activity areas. Garages, parking spaces, walkways, and even outdoor storage areas are examples of utility zones that are often nearby gardens. Because they are seldom used on a continuous basis, grasses and small shrubs have more time to recover from damage. Trees are not often planted in these zones, and therefore the threat to their habitat is greatly reduced.

The aesthetic area is where the plant material can thrive and remain virtually undisturbed by human intrusion. It is possible not to venture into this portion of the garden at all and still enjoy its serenity.

An excellent example of an aesthetic area, this garden space is effective because it is undisturbed by human intrusion.

A simple pathway through a planted area allows people to use the space without damaging the plant materials.

Natural-looking boardwalks allow people and plant materials mutual space without restricting aesthetic qualities.

This zone is developed just to be seen from a distance and not to walk into. If designed on this basis, the palette of sensitive plants in this area can be greatly increased to expand the beauty of the wild garden.

Before you begin planning your garden, be sure to identify the amount of space you will need for each of these areas. Take the total square feet you have to work with and select the functional zones as needed. You may wish to place the more sensitive areas (utility and aesthetic) farther away from the buildings.

Clearings allow circulation into this space without treading on the delicate groundcover.

Some groundcover masses function as visual elements and are best appreciated from afar.

As with some works of art, a close-up look at this groundcover mass would lessen its appeal. It is best to view this aesthetic area at a distance to fully capture its visual essence.

A natural blending of groundcover masses and grass will allow the gardener to venture into this garden space without fear of damaging plants.

Flowers along the edge of a stream reflect pleasingly into the water to magnify the aesthetic effect.

THE PLANTING ELEMENTS

As with the ornamental garden, the wild composition needs to be organized—not in the form of clipped hedges and finely divided plant masses, but in the associations of one plant group to another. While the emphasis in the contemporary garden is on the spaces created by plants, the wild garden should emphasize the plants and not the spaces they create.

A sculpture garden, for instance, relies upon the trimmed hedge to provide a controlled backdrop for the artwork displayed. In the wild garden, the plant mass becomes the work of art displaying nature's creative endeavors. A chosen space for a patio or utility area may become overgrown with a particular plant or group of plants. If this occurs, remember that wild plants have the "right of way" in the natural composition, and only selective management should be employed to control the plant's growth. Wholesale mowing or trimming should be avoided.

In this reversal of commonly accepted roles, people and their needs are subordinate to the needs of wild plants. That is to say, people should place their trust in the aesthetic sensibilities of nature and let the native garden plants serve as the dominant element.

The basic design elements of any garden composition are *plant color, form,* and *texture.* When applied to outdoor areas, these elements create balance, accent, scale, and specific sequential patterns, which form a cohesive outdoor environment. In a typical landscape, the bright colors of massed flowers identify entries and walkways. Well-trimmed shrubs outline boundaries between one lawn and another. Large trees provide shade, also giving a predominant appearance of control and order.

Within the wild garden, however, the basic laws of man's landscape designs are not so rigid. Nature plants and directs the grasses, shrubs, and trees into the locations best suited for their survival. If the masses create specific colors, forms, or textures to enhance a scenic view, it is merely coincidental. If bright colors appear as an accent feature, it is because the environmental conditions are there to create them. Therefore, an attractive wild garden is the result of accommodating the gardener's needs and desires to the natural planting laws.

Massive stone outcroppings add background accents to a myriad of seasonal colors.

Delicate phlox plants cover this forest floor and wash the open area with a tint of light blue.

Delicate trillium *will make a subtle accent for a secluded aesthetic area.*

Color

A garden does not have to depend upon ornamental flowers to achieve bright accent colors. Indeed, these annual bloomers cannot provide the continuous colors often found in the natural environment of a wild garden. Instead of bright, flashy, color patterns dominating for brief periods of time, the colors in the wild composition are more subtle and lasting. Colors gradually change from month to month, often so subtly as to seem imperceptible.

As seasons progress, so do the color variations. The warm spring hues of flowering shrubs, small trees, and grasses may appear within hidden masses of vines or understory. When sprinkled with other accents, such as tangled twigs and fast growing vines, the landscape composition becomes more tranquil and enjoyable.

When summer arrives, the greenish colorations begin to wash the entire landscape with accents. The overstory of a forest garden may be dark and dominated by light-filtering shapes. These trees will blend into the lighter greens of the understory and taller shrub areas. The herbs and grasses add bright greens for luster,

and the final summer sequences are there for the gardener's delight.

Fall offers the most spectacular time for the enjoyment of wild-garden color. As the temperatures fall and the crisp air surrounds the native plants, their dormancy period begins. It is at this time that the reds and yellows and oranges and browns begin to show their splendor. For a few weeks each year, this design element has been naturally arranged and we are allowed to enjoy its beauty. By planning ahead and paying close attention to your plants' needs, you can ensure that color will become a major aesthetic feature of your wild garden.

Form

Form is the shape and structure of a plant or plant mass, an element that will change very little as the seasons pass. The dominant shapes, when viewed from a distance, will be characteristically round or oval for deciduous plants, and triangular for evergreen varieties. During the winter months, the intricate structure of an overhead canopy will add elegance and interest to views from within the garden. Rounded masses of smaller shrubs will expose the abandoned bird's nest unnoticed during the leafy summer.

Always take advantage of a plant's natural form. Never trim or clip a plant to force it into a desired shape. You may, of course, practice selective trimming if a fallen limb or leaning tree is precariously situated or encroaching on someone else's property. Remember, though, that natural shapes and structures are the goals for the wild garden. Manicured features and growth control are only for the ornamental landscape garden.

Different garden themes may emphasize different plant forms. In the forest garden, for instance, with its many trees and large shrubs, form will be a major design element. The meadow garden, on the other hand, may have few noticeable varieties in plant form other than those of the rounded grass and shrub clumps. The water garden may contain only the subtle forms of the floating aquatics or the background forms of the marginal aquatics.

Blended masses of native and ornamental plants dominate the garden composition.

This lava rock hillside is accentuated with rounded succulents of varying colors and textures. The small pockets of sand and soil between the stones are stabilizing factors that sustain this approach to a wild composition.

Even in winter, an individual mass of plants will give character to the landscape since snow will accentuate its graceful form.

This cascading groundcover provides a blanket for the exposed hillside rock.

The diversity of this garden feature is exemplified by wood ferns at the water's edge and yuccas among the outcroppings of stone.

A vignette of boulders and groundcover exemplifies effective usage of natural elements.

Texture

Wild-garden textures are mutable. At close investigation, the predominant texture may be the unique fineness of individual plant leaves or the single blades of a clump of grass. From a distance, a group of plants may create an entirely different textural effect than from close range.

Sunrises and sunsets, and the hours in between, will also vary the patterns of texture in your wild composition. Different times of the day will cast shadows onto the plant masses and expand the visual appearance of this design element.

In the forest garden, texture will be evident primarily in the overstory zone, with splashes of other textures throughout the shrub and groundcover layer as well. Interesting tree-bark characteristics can also be used to create textural accents. The meadow garden will be predominantly "smoother" in appearance because the grasses and small shrubs do not have conspicuous textures. The water garden can add a bit more textural variety, as rough-appearing plants are set off against a backdrop of mirror-smooth pools of water.

The functional applications of groundcovers, baffles, and canopy zones are evident in this woodland garden.

THE FUNCTIONAL MASSES

The functional arrangement of your natural landscape may be the same as that of an ornamental composition. The architectural devices of walls, ceilings, and floors are used to create the spatial elements you need for your property. Garden walls, for instance, are comprised of *baffles, barriers,* and *screens.* Ceilings are made up of *canopies* and floors of *groundcovers.* The spatial functions of your wild garden are determined by these components. They should be used to establish the activity, utility, and aesthetic areas of your space.

Wall elements should act as the vertical control features of your garden. When undesirable views occur off-site, a screening mass of small to medium shrubs and seedling trees should be planted. They will block the view and direct attention to more attractive features. A baffle mass may be used to obstruct only part of the view. Partially hidden splashes of wild-flower color make unexpected and attractive visual features that accent the garden.

Barrier plantings prevent people from walking where they are not welcome. Sensitive plants need protection, for people can harm the delicate balance of the vegetation communities. Use this wall element for control, and to direct visitors to specific locations within the garden.

Canopies and groundcovers are the horizontal control features of the design. If an interesting leaf pattern exists on a large shade tree, an exciting visual experience will be created as one looks upward toward the canopy feature.

Groundcovers stimulate the visual experiences that will occur below eye level. Variegated patterns of groundcover can be accomplished by using different species of grasses and small shrubs. A fallen tree or stone outcropping can complete the composition in an imaginative fashion.

GRASSES AND FORBS CAN FUNCTION AS THE VISUAL FLOOR	DENSE SHRUB MASSES CAN FUNCTION AS A BARRIER	UNDERSTORY TREES CAN FUNCTION AS A BAFFLE OR SCREEN	THE OVERSTORY CAN FUNCTION AS A CANOPY	LARGE DENSE SHRUBS CAN FUNCTION AS A SCREEN	WILD FLOWERS CAN FUNCTION AS A GROUNDCOVER

CANOPY ZONE

BAFFLE OR SCREEN ZONE

GROUNDCOVER

The wild forms of plants that will comprise the structures of the natural-landscape garden consist of mosses and lichens, shrubs and herbs, seedling trees, understory trees, and overstory (canopy) trees.

The use of irregular masses of annual flowers among partially exposed stones adds an unusually beautiful character to this forest floor.

HOW TO GET YOUR GARDEN STARTED

Developing a wild-garden theme is like developing any other landscape composition—it takes patience and planning to ensure the proper arrangement of plant materials. Unlike the ornamental garden, however, natural-landscape materials must be arranged according to their natural habitat and environmental needs, which do not always coincide with the needs of the homeowner. The following steps will assist you in developing the composition of your wild garden.

Step One:
Identify the Planting Region

Determine in which one of the thirty-two plant growth regions your garden is located. This step will establish basic environmental needs in your garden. For instance, if you live in Region 1 (North Pacific Coast) you will not be able to develop a theme characteristic of Region 32 (Subtropical Florida). Environmental conditions will not allow the plant materials from these two regions to mix. Adjacent regions, however, are often compatible, and a mixing of both plants and habitat conditions may be possible. (See page 17 for the Plant Growth Regions of North America.)

If your garden has a woodland or meadow theme, compare your regions to the specific types of forest and grassland communities of North America. This comparison will establish your basic list of plant materials. If you plan to develop a water garden, consult the Precipitation chart on page 15. Then, use the information from the charts for a consultation at a native plant society to find out exactly which plants will thrive in your region.

Step Two:
Select the Functional Masses

In order to make a selection of plants for each theme you should be familiar with the general masses that apply to each garden theme. Each wild-garden area will have the following mass characteristics:

1. The woodland garden will consist primarily of *ceilings* (tall and medium-height trees) and *floors* (groundcovers of small shrubs, ivies, and shade-loving flowers). Plant-material selection should emphasize these functional characteristics. Although wall elements may occur, the forest canopy and the forest floor will be the important areas to consider.

2. The meadow garden will consist primarily of *floors* (groundcovers of grasses, small shrubs, and wild flowers) and *walls* (medium to tall shrubs). If a sun-filled meadow is your objective, the ceiling element (canopy) should be almost totally absent from your garden. To maintain the open effect, emphasize grasses, small shrubs, and wild flowers.

3. The water garden will consist primarily of *floors* (grasses, water-loving shrubs, and flowers) and *walls* (small to medium shrubs). Shade elements over the water garden will promote algae and excessive moss development, so ceiling elements should be virtually nonexistent. Plant-material selection should be limited to masses that promote a pleasing view of the garden.

A pathway journeys alongside a water feature with marginal aquatic plants that accent the edge. Large shrubs and canopy elements blend together to form a useful screen.

This meadow theme blends well with a water feature that is enhanced by the yellow flag iris.

Step Three:
Collect Wild Plants

The task of gathering and collecting wild plants is much easier today than it was just a few short years ago. Wild gardens have become very desirable because of their practical effects upon the home environment. Less energy is expended to maintain nonornamental plants, and nature has provided an extensive supply of natural beauty in the environment.

Plant selection for the wild garden should begin at the local nursery. Although many of the available plant materials will be ornamental varieties, you should find some native species in stock, especially trees. Shade trees (the large canopy species) are the most readily available from local sources. And if they are not in stock, most establishments will plan a collected trip for those homeowners who are willing to wait for the exact tree that fits their needs.

Small shrubs and grasses are not as easy to find at a nursery. Some of the popular shrubs will be bare-rooted and can only be planted during certain periods of the year. Your local garden supplier will know best about the specific planting times for a particular species. Grasses can best be grown from seeds. Fortunately, many seed companies are now providing native grass-seed varieties in convenient packages just for wild-garden environments. Some commercial seed catalogs are even selling wild-grass seeds suitable for many areas in North America. (Several commercial sources of wild flowers and grasses are listed in the appendix section for easy reference.)

Locate your plant materials from the following:

1. Local nurseries and garden centers.
2. Commercial seed companies and catalogs.
3. Local and regional plant societies.
4. Public and private gardens.
5. University plant collections.
6. Native habitats existing in your area.

And keep in mind these helpful tips:

- Study the planting regions in your area.
- Consider *your* needs *before* selecting the functional masses.
- Attempt to duplicate the plants' native habitat.
- Don't select plants before studying your plant region.
- Never collect wild plants from their natural habitat before asking about other sources first.
- Check with local plant experts for appropriate times to plant your garden.
- Consider subscribing to *The Natural Garden Newsletter*, 3015 Woodsdale Boulevard, Lincoln, NE 68502-5053. This publication will help you tend your garden all year long.

These native wild flowers are more prevalent today because of the demand for their use in wild compositions.

This natural pond is a good source for collecting wild aquatic plants.

Snowdrops emerge from a blanket of decomposing leaves and small twigs in this forest composition.

Characteristic Plants for Wild-Garden Themes

For the Woodland Garden...

	TREES		UNDERGROWTH	
THE NORTH AMERICAN DECIDUOUS FOREST	American Beech American Holly Black Walnut Bur Oak Chestnut Oak Common Chokecherry Hackberry Hemlock Mockernut Hickory	Post Oak Red Maple Slippery Elm Sugar Maple Sugarberry Swamp Chestnut Oak White Basswood White Pine Yellow Buckeye	Bloodroot Common Nettle Jewelweed Pawpaw	Spicebush Squirrel Corn Stemless Wild Ginger Waterleaf
THE FLOODPLAIN FOREST	American Hornbeam Box Elder Cherrybark Oak Cottonwood Green Ash Persimmon	Pignut Hickory Sandbar Willow Southern Red Oak Sugarmaple Sweetgum Sycamore	Cat Briar Climbing Bittersweet Gooseberry Herbaceous Mandrake Homewort Pawpaw	Red Bud Smooth Ruellia Spicebush Trumpet Vine Virginia Creeper Virginia Knotweed
THE BOREAL CONIFEROUS FOREST	Aspen Balsam Spruce Black Spruce Jack Pine	Mountain Maple Paper Birch Red Spruce White Spruce	Bunchberry Labrador Tea Mountain Ash Sour Top Bilberry	Speckled Alder Sweet-Scented Bed Straw Twinflower Wild Sarsaparilla
THE MONTANE CONIFEROUS FOREST AND ALPINE COMMUNITIES	Blue Spruce· Bristlecone Pine Douglas Fir Engelmann Spruce	Limber Pine Lodgepole Pine Ponderosa Pine Subalpine Fir	Blueberry Dearberry Dogwood Mountain Ash	Ninebark Oak Bush Soapberry Squashberry
THE NORTHERN PACIFIC COAST– RAINY WESTERN HEMLOCK FOREST	Black Cottonwood Douglas Fir Red Alder Grand Fir	Sitka Spruce Western Cedar Western Hemlock Western Larch	Cream Bush Devil's Club Oregon Grape Red Bilberry	Salal Salmon-berry Vine Maple Waxberry
THE BROAD SCLEROPHYLL– GRIZZLY BEAR COMMUNITY	Bigleaf Maple Blue Oak California Black Oak California Laurel	Digger Pine Douglas Fir Garry Oak Tan Oak	Canyon Live Oak Catchfly Filaree Interior Live Oak	Popcorn Flower Sumac Tarweed Turkey Mullein

Characteristic Plants for Wild-Garden Themes

For the Meadow Garden...

	GROUNDCOVERS	
EASTERN PRAIRIE EDGE	Butterfly Weed Colic Root Common Milkweed False Heather Hairgrass	Horseweed Indian Hemp Partridge Pea Poverty Grass Sundrops
TALL- AND MIXED-GRASS PRAIRIES	Big Bluestem Broomweed Buffalo Grass Green Needlegrass Junegrass Little Bluestem Needle-and-Thread Grass Panic Grass	Porcupine Grass Prairie Dropseed Ragweed Sand Dropseed Scurf-Pea Side-Oats Grama Slender Wheatgrass Sunflower
SHORT-GRASS PRAIRIE	Blue Grama Buffalo Grass Goldenrod June Grass Little Bluestem	Poverty Three-Awn Grass Ragweed Side-Oats Grama Silver Beardgrass Sunflower
COASTAL PRAIRIE	Big Bluestem Buffalo Grass Hairy Tridens	Little Bluestem Smut-Grass Texas Needlegrass
BUNCH-GRASS DESERT SHRUB	Common Chokecherry Greenleaf Manzanita Huckleberry Oak Mountain Mahogany	Snow Bush Squaw Bush Sumac Wavyleaf Oak
SAGEBRUSH GRASSLAND	Black Bush Black Sage Bud Sage Buckwheat Greasewood Mexican Tea	Rice Grass Sagebush Saltbush Shadscale Slat-Blite Winter-Fat
CALIFORNIA GRASSLAND	California Poppy Fowl Meadow Grass Idaho Fescue	Rough-Stalked Meadow Grass Wood Meadow Grass

For the Water Garden

The numbers following plant names indicate to what water features they are best suited:

1 = SPRING
2 = POND
3 = SMALL LAKE

PERIMETER PLANTINGS	Bald **2,3** Basket Willow **1, 2, 3** Cattail **1, 2, 3** Rattlesnake Fern **1, 2** Water Poppy **1, 2**
MARGINAL AQUATICS	Basket Willow **2, 3** Cattail **2, 3** Umbrella Plant **2, 3**
FLOATING AQUATICS	Duckweed **2, 3** Mosquito Fern **2, 3**
DEEP AQUATICS	Coontail **3** Fish Grass **2, 3** Floating Fern **2, 3** Royal Water Lily **3** Water Fern **2, 3** White Water Lily **3** Yellow Water Lily **3**

WILD-GARDEN AMENITIES

ATTRACTING WILDLIFE

The wild-garden composition is more than plants alone. It is an organization of associated communities of both plants and animals. Each species has its specific ecological niche, and each has its unique effect upon the quality of the natural garden space.

Wild animals are as much a part of the natural landscape as the rosebush is to the urban or suburban garden. You'll find that, whatever your wild-garden theme, an array of beautiful creatures will be readily attracted to the tranquil habitat you've helped create.

As you select a specific seed-clustering grass for your meadow or a berry-ladened understory for your forest, you establish a very basic food element that will attract animals to the space—not an artifical food dispenser that scatters seeds throughout the landscape, but very specific food sources for very specific wildlife.

Some birds, for instance, have a fondness for particular types of foods. They often travel many miles just for their favorite staple. To attract these species to a garden, it is important to include the host plants in your design. Avoid feeding with supplemental containers that attract all kinds of birds. These commercial feeding products will create an imbalance of wildlife. Too many birds creates feeding pressure on your garden plants and may inhibit their development.

Nesting habitat is also crucial to a well-balanced garden. Small twigs and branches will become structural components for nesting wildlife. Grasses will make excellent cover for both birds and small mammals. Tree stumps and rock outcroppings will also make convenient sanctuaries for numerous creatures.

A bearded gobbler will make a rare and exciting visitor to any wild garden

The squirrel is one of the first residents of a wild garden.

Birds for the Garden

In addition to the more common city-dweller species of birds found in typical ornamental gardens, the following species of birds may be attracted to your home environment with the development of a wild-garden theme.

For the Woodland Garden...

BLACK-THROATED GRAY WARBLER
Likes shrubby open areas in coniferous forest gardens and in some deciduous gardens. Mostly found in the forests extending from western New Mexico to south British Columbia.

CEDAR WAXWING
Likes the forest edges, where natural fruiting trees are found. Found from coast to coast in mixed-forest areas.

DOWNY WOODPECKER
Likes mixed forest areas (pines and deciduous trees) but nests mostly in young seedling trees. Found in most of North America except the hot desert areas of New Mexico and Arizona.

GOSHAWK
Likes the northern coniferous forests and some areas of the prairie regions from Maine to New Mexico, and northward into Alaska and the Canadian Rockies.

HOUSE WREN
Likes deciduous forests. Found throughout North America, from Mexico to all southern Canadian provinces.

NORTHERN SHRIKE
Likes pine forests and some open areas with tree edges. Found in areas north of a line stretching from southern Oregon to New Jersey.

PYGMY OWL
Likes open pine forests with canyons and large trees. Found in most forest areas in the Rockies from New Mexico to British Columbia, northern Alberta, and Alaska.

TURKEY
Likes forest areas with oaks and other deciduous materials. Found in the forest areas of the eastern and southwestern United States.

WHIPPOORWILL
Likes pine and deciduous forest areas. Prefers eastern forest areas from Texas to Maine, and the southernmost portions of New Mexico.

For the Meadow Garden...

BOBWHITE
Likes the forest edges where small open meadows appear. Found in the foothills of the Rocky Mountains eastward to southern New York.

BURROWING OWL
Likes open areas with small sagebrushlike vegetation. Found in most western states from Texas northward into Canada, and westward to all the Pacific states.

COMMON NIGHTHAWK
Likes open grassy areas and similar gardens. Roosts in small edge trees and on fenceposts. Found in most areas of North America except southern California.

EASTERN MEADOWLARK
Likes open grasslands with brushy borders. Found from southeast Canada, east across United States to Arizona.

LUCY'S WARBLER
Likes the areas along streams and shrubby meadows. Found in most desertlike areas of the Southwest.

ROADRUNNER
Likes the more arid gardens, such as the chaparral vegetation of southwestern areas. Found in much of the Southwest, into Colorado and western Louisiana.

For the Water Garden...

CATTLE EGRET

Likes marshy pastures but will roost in wooded areas. Found in the southern lowlands of California to Texas and along the Gulf Coast states into New Jersey.

COMMON SNIPE

Likes marshes and boggy areas. Found in most of North America, including all provinces of Canada.

GREAT EGRET

Likes deep-water marshes with vegetation on the banks. May nest in cattails. Does not like extremely cold climates or desert areas.

LEAST TERN

Likes beach areas of shallow water along rivers, lakes, and coasts. Found near most major rivers in North America and as far north as British Columbia.

MARSH HAWK

Likes marshes and meadows near low-water areas, where water is only a few feet deep. Found in most of North America.

RED-WINGED BLACKBIRD

Likes marshy areas but will move into meadow areas that are near water. Found throughout North America.

These are just a few of the hundreds of unique species of birds you can attract to your wild-garden area. For more information about specific species in your region, contact your local USDA Extension Agent or consult one of the many field guides to the birds of North America.

A protruding boulder provides a sunny resting spot for the resident of a wild water garden.

A well-planted wild garden and properly developed water feature will attract even the solitary great blue heron.

Wildlife for the Garden

Not only birds are attracted to wild-garden themes—many other kinds of wildlife also thrive in forest, meadow, and wetland environments.

For the Woodland Garden . . .

BEE
The honeybee is attracted to woodlands by basswood, redbud tree, red maple, and aster.

BUTTERFLY
Attracted by poplar, ash, and elm.

CHIPMUNK
Both the eastern and western chipmunks prefer to live in wooded areas and live on nuts, fruits, and berries. They will often hide in stumps and rotting trees.

DEER
The white-tailed deer is found across North America in woodland areas and occasionally in pastures.

FOX SQUIRREL
Found from the midwestern regions eastward, this species favors oaks and nut-bearing trees.

GRAY SQUIRREL
The western gray squirrel is partial to oaks and nut-bearing plants such as the yew and holly.

For the Meadow Garden . . .

BEE
In meadows, the honeybee is attracted to white clover and the bumblebee is attracted to red clover. A mix of wild flowers in varied colors will also draw these useful insects into your meadow environment.

BUTTERFLY
Always a delightful addition to the wild composition, the butterfly is attracted to meadows by clover, milkweed, butterfly weed, aster, grasses, joe-pye weed, goldenrod, and the coneflower.

GARTER SNAKE
This useful reptile will prey on garden pests.

RABBIT
There are many species of rabbits found across North America. They all enjoy eating grasses, and will eat the bark off of yew, hemlock, and evergreen plants.

For the Water Garden . . .

KINGSNAKE
Although not a threat to human beings, this reptile will eat other harmful snakes and consume pesky rodents.

MUSKRAT
These fascinating mammals will make their homes at a pond's edge and take swims in the water.

ROCKS AND STONES

Once plant materials mature, both natural and constructed stone outcroppings become even more attractive wild-garden features.

Rocks and stones should be placed at different levels to allow water features to develop more visual focal points.

Outcroppings of small stones or large boulders provide attractive accents to the wild garden. They are important elements for giving a finished character to the space. Not only will they retain soil masses and prevent erosion, but they will also help divide one usable space from another.

Natural arrangements of stone can sep-

arate an activity area from an aesthetic area and limit access, to protect sensitive native plants. Stone arrangements can be used to develop areas of higher ground and can also function as pathways, particularly in sodden areas. Some plant species will only grow on or near rocks or large boulders. Brightly colored lichens and mosses on large natural stone ar-

rangements provide a completed link to the plant chain.

These features should be placed in an informal arrangement. Never use two boulders of identical size or an abundance of similar materials. Make sure rocks are located properly for soil pockets to accumulate. This extra step provides a base for plants that grow on stone faces.

Left: To create an interesting interplay between two distinct garden styles, individual masses of native plant materials are used within this ornamental composition. **Below top:** Moss-covered stones and fallen trees provide the base for this pathway through a prairie hillside. **Below bottom:** Grasses and blooming groundcovers provide a carpeted cover for this functional entry feature. The large boulders are lightly covered with lichens to represent the lower end of the natural plant forms.

STUMPS AND OLD TREES

Unlike ornamental gardens, the wild landscape should not be devoid of rotten tree stumps, fallen trees, or even old and nearly dead trees. If these elements occur naturally in your garden do not remove them. An old tree with dead limbs need not be pruned. Instead, the effect of the weathered and gnarled wood among the high grasses, uninhibited growths of wildflowers, and other attractive wildgarden features will look right at home. Additionally, old trees provide perfect home sites for wildlife.

Old trees will also make ideal locations for birdfeeders and birdhouses, should you choose to add them to the garden. When a tree is decaying or is partially hollowed, the conditions are perfect for a variety of cavity-nesting birds and mammals to move in and create a home. More than one species will often nest in the same tree, provided it is large enough. Among the species found in such situations are woodpeckers, chickadees, bluebirds, screech owls, and titmice.

Allow fallen trees to continue to decay for they add valuable compost materials for the other neighboring plants. As the wood deteriorates, insects will move in and make their home in the materials. This, in turn, attracts wildlife that feed on the insects. Chipmunks, for example, enjoy fallen trees and their stumps as hiding places.

Fallen trees can act as log pathways and are particularly useful when traipsing through wetland gardens.

By using these suggestions and incorporating natural elements into your wildgarden theme, you will be able to create a spectacular, personalized garden that will provide pleasure for years to come.

Fallen trees are often removed from the ornamental garden because of their unsightly appearance. In the wild garden, they are an integral part of the composition.

Cascading waterfalls through old tree stumps are an outstanding accent for a wild garden.

Even as trees die and fall across groundcover masses, they should be left undisturbed so the natural garden character can be maintained.

Above top, bottom: *Weathered stumps should remain a part of the wild-garden composition. They provide homes for insects, which in turn attract birds and small animals into the landscape.*

RESOURCES

WHERE TO VISIT WILD GARDENS

The concept of wild-garden development has emerged only recently. Just a few years ago, use of native plants in a garden was frowned upon and avoided. Fortunately, however, this attitude has changed, and plant lovers are taking more time to enjoy the beauty of wild materials. The careful selection of specialized species is now at the top of our lists, with clipped hedges occupying space at the bottom.

Visualizing a finished wild garden is a major stumbling block for the average gardener. Few completed projects exist in our neighborhoods, and the "natural" parks of our local cities are usually nothing more than unkempt land holdings. So the following list of wild-garden projects may be of assistance to you. Your local Soil Conservation Service and Cooperative Extension Service may also have a list of completed projects in your area.

To study individual plants and the associations of these materials to their species communities, you may wish to visit . . .

United States

BELLINGRATH GARDENS
Theodore, Alabama

UNIVERSITY OF CALIFORNIA BOTANICAL GARDENS
Berkeley, California

DENVER BOTANICAL GARDENS
Denver, Colorado

GREENWICH AUDUBON CENTER
Greenwich, Connecticut

PLATT HILL PARK
Winchester, Connecticut

SLEEPING GIANT STATE PARK
Hamden, Connecticut

NATIONAL ARBORETUM
Washington, D.C.

GOOSE LAKE PRAIRIE STATE PARK
Morris, Illinois

ILLINOIS BEACH STATE PARK
Waukegan, Illinois

SHAWNEE NATIONAL FOREST
Harrisburg, Illinois

HOOSIER PRAIRIE
Highland, Indiana

INDIANA DUNES NATIONAL LAKESHORE
Michigan City, Indiana

SPRING MILL STATE PARK
Lawrenceport, Indiana

BICKELHAUPT ARBORETUM
Clinton, Iowa

HAYDEN PRAIRIE
Saratoga, Iowa

UNIVERSITY OF NORTHERN IOWA
Cedar Falls, Iowa (entire campus)

WAUBONSIE STATE PARK
Waubonsie, Iowa

DANIEL BOONE NATIONAL FOREST
Winchester, Kentucky

MAMMOTH CAVE NATIONAL PARK
Brownsville, Kentucky

ACADIA NATIONAL PARK
Bar Harbor, Maine

BEAR SWAMP RESERVATION
Ashfield, Massachusetts

PHILLIPS ANDOVER SUCCESSION PROJECT
Charles Ward Reservation
Andover, Massachusetts

WESTFIELD RIVER WILDERNESS
Hampshire County, Massachusetts

W. J. BEAL BOTANICAL GARDEN
Michigan State University
East Lansing, Michigan

MANISTER NATIONAL FOREST
Cadillac, Michigan

MICHIGAN NATURE ASSOCIATION
Avoca, Michigan

PICTURED ROCKS NATIONAL LAKESHORE
Munising, Michigan

LAKE ITASCA STATE PARK
Park Rapids, Minnesota

GLACIAL LAKE STATE PARK
Starbuck, Minnesota

ST. LOUIS BOTANICAL GARDENS
St. Louis, Missouri

BROOKLYN BOTANICAL GARDENS
Brooklyn, New York

CENTRAL PARK
Schenectady, New York

AULLWOOD AUDUBON CENTER
Dayton, Ohio

THE WILDERNESS
Adams County, Ohio

ALLEGHENY NATIONAL FOREST
Warren, Pennsylvania

BOWMAN'S HILL WILDFLOWER PRESERVE
Washington Crossing Park, Pennsylvania

PRESQUE ISLE STATE PARK
Erie, Pennsylvania

JOHN TYLER ARBORETUM
Lima, Pennsylvania

FORT WORTH BOTANICAL GARDEN
Fort Worth, Texas

HOUSTON ARBORETUM AND BOTANICAL GARDENS
Houston, Texas

WHITE MOUNTAIN NATIONAL FOREST
Waterville, Vermont

JEFFERSON NATIONAL FOREST
Roanoke, Virginia

SHENANDOAH NATIONAL PARK
Front Royal, Virginia

CORE ARBORETUM
Morgantown, West Virginia

BOERNER BOTANICAL GARDENS
Hales Corners, Wisconsin

NECEDAH WILDLIFE REFUGE
Necedah, Wisconsin

THE UNIVERSITY OF WISCONSIN ARBORETUM
Madison, Wisconsin

Canada

NATIONAL PARKS

AUYUITTUQ NATIONAL PARK
Pangnirtung, Northwest
 Territories
X0A 0R0

BANFF NATIONAL PARK
Box 900
Banff, Alberta
T0L 0C0

CAPE BRETON HIGHLANDS NATIONAL PARK
Ingonish Beach
Cape Breton, Nova Scotia
B0X 1L0

ELK ISLAND NATIONAL PARK
R.R. 1
Fort Saskatchewan, Alberta
T8L 2N7

FORILLON NATIONAL PARK
Box 1220
Gaspé, Québec
G0C 1R0

FUNDY NATIONAL PARK
Alma, New Brunswick
E0A 1B0

GEORGIAN BAY ISLANDS NATIONAL PARK
Box 28
Honey Harbour, Ontario
P0E 1E0

GRASSLANDS NATIONAL PARK
Val Marie, Saskatchewan
S0N 2T0

GROS MORNE NATIONAL PARK
Box 130
Rocky Harbour,
 Newfoundland
A0K 4N0

JASPER NATIONAL PARK
Box 10
Jasper, Alberta
T0E 1E0

KEJIMKUJIK NATIONAL PARK
Box 36
Maitland Bridge
Annapolis County, Nova
 Scotia
B0T 1N0

KLUANE NATIONAL PARK
Haines Junction, Yukon
 Territory
Y0B 1L0

KOOTENAY NATIONAL PARK
Box 220
Radium Hot Springs, British
 Columbia
V0A 1M0

KOUCHIBOUGUAC NATIONAL PARK
Kouchibouguac, New
 Brunswick
E0A 2A0

LA MAURICIE NATIONAL PARK
C.P. 758
465 Fifth Street
Shawinigan, Québec
G9N 6V9

MOUNT REVELSTOKE AND GLACIER NATIONAL PARKS
Box 350
Revelstoke, British Columbia
V0E 2S0

NAHANNI NATIONAL PARK
Box 300
Fort Simpson, Northwest
 Territories
X0E 0N0

PACIFIC RIM NATIONAL PARK
Box 280
Ucluelet, British Columbia
V0R 3A0

POINT PELEE NATIONAL PARK
R.R. 1
Leamington, Ontario
N8H 3V4

PRINCE ALBERT NATIONAL PARK
Box 100
Waskesiu Lake, Saskatchewan
S0J 2Y0

PRINCE EDWARD ISLAND NATIONAL PARK
Box 487
Charlottetown, Prince Edward
 Island
C1A 7L1

PUKASKWA NATIONAL PARK
Box 550
Marathon, Ontario
P0T 2E0

RIDING MOUNTAIN NATIONAL PARK
Wasagaming, Manitoba
R0J 2H0

ST. LAWRENCE ISLANDS NATIONAL PARK
Box 469
R.R. 3
Mallorytown Landing, Ontario
K0E 1R0

TERRA NOVA NATIONAL PARK
Glovertown, Newfoundland
A0G 2L0

WATERTON LAKES NATIONAL PARK
Waterton Park, Alberta
T0K 2M0

WOOD BUFFALO NATIONAL PARK
Box 750
Fort Smith, Northwest
 Territories
X0E 0P0

YOHO NATIONAL PARK
Box 99
Field, British Columbia
V0A 1G0

PUBLIC GARDENS

BUTCHARD GARDENS
Victoria, British Columbia

DOMINIUM ARBORETUM
Ottawa, Ontario

EDWARDS GARDENS
Toronto, Ontario

HUMBER ARBORETUM
Rexdale, Ontario

MONTREAL BOTANICAL GARDEN
Montreal, Quebec

NIAGARA PARK COMMISSION SCHOOL OF HORTICULTURE
Niagara Falls, Ontario

QUEEN ELIZABETH GARDENS
Vancouver, British Columbia

ROYAL BOTANICAL GARDENS
Hamilton, Ontario

NATIVE PLANT SOCIETIES

Finding what you need for your wild-garden theme is much easier today than just a few short years ago. Once only the dedicated enthusiast could locate that special grass clump or seedling tree. Collecting plants in the open country was difficult, and seeds of some unusual species were unavailable outside the scientific laboratory.

Today, native plant species are finding their way into local nursery stocks, and commercial seed companies ship adaptable varieties all over the country. Native plant societies are organizing local chapters to encourage this new trend and provide assistance when necessary.

If you are unable to make that countryside trip to collect the plants you need, you may wish to contact one of the following organizations for assistance.

United States

ARIZONA NATIVE PLANT SOCIETY
530 East Cambridge Drive
Tucson, AZ 85704

ARKANSAS NATIVE PLANT SOCIETY
Route 1, Box 282
Mena, AR 71953

CALIFORNIA NATIVE PLANT SOCIETY
2380 Ellsworth Street
Berkeley, CA 94704

COLORADO NATIVE PLANT SOCIETY
Box 200
Ft. Collins, CO 80522

FLORIDA NATIVE PLANT SOCIETY
1203 Orange Avenue
Winter Park, FL 32789

GEORGIA BOTANICAL SOCIETY
Route 1
Tiger, GA 30576

HAWAII BOTANICAL SOCIETY
Native Plant Committee
Botany Department
University of Hawaii
Honolulu, HI 96822

IDAHO NATIVE PLANT SOCIETY
Box 9451
Boise, ID 83707

MICHIGAN BOTANICAL CLUB
Botany Department
Michigan State University
East Lansing, MI 48823

MISSOURI NATIVE PLANT SOCIETY
Department of Conservation
Box 180
Jefferson City, MO 65101

NEVADA NATIVE PLANT SOCIETY
Box 8965
Reno, NV 89507

NEW MEXICO NATIVE PLANT SOCIETY
Box 5917
Santa Fe, NM 87502

NORTH CAROLINA WILDFLOWER PRESERVATION SOCIETY
North Carolina Botanical Garden
Chapel Hill, NC 27514

OKLAHOMA NATIVE PLANT SOCIETY
Route 1, Box 157
Durant, OK 74701

OREGON NATIVE PLANT SOCIETY
393 Fulvue Drive
Eugene, OR 97405

TENNESSEE NATIVE PLANT SOCIETY
Botany Department
University of Tennessee
Knoxville, TN 37916

TEXAS NATIVE PLANT SOCIETY
Box 23836, TWU Station
Denton, TX 76204

UTAH NATIVE PLANT SOCIETY
Utah State Arboretum
University of Utah
Salt Lake City, UT 84112

WASHINGTON NATIVE PLANT SOCIETY
Botany Department
University of Washington
Seattle, WA 98195

WYOMING NATIVE PLANT SOCIETY
1603 Capitol Avenue
Cheyenne, WY 82001

Canada

ALBERTA HORTICULTURAL ASSOCIATION
Box 223
Lacombe, Alberta T0C 1S0

BRITISH COLUMBIA COUNCIL OF GARDEN CLUBS
10595 Dunlop Road
Delta, British Columbia V4C 7G2

CANADIAN BOTANICAL ASSOCIATION
Department of Botany
University of British Columbia
Vancouver, British Columbia
V6T 2B1

CANADIAN HOBBY GREENHOUSE ASSOCIATION
83-270 Timberbank Boulevard
Agincourt, Ontario M1W 2M1

CANADIAN PARKS/RECREATION ASSOCIATION
Association Canadienne des Loisirs/Parcs
333 River Road
Vanier, Ontario K1L 8H9

CANADIAN WILDFLOWER SOCIETY
35 Bauer Crescent
Unionville, Ontario L3R 4H3

FÉDÉRATION DES SOCIÉTÉS D'HORTICULTURE ET D'ÉCOLOGIE DU QUÉBEC
1415 rue Jarry est
Montreal, Quebec H2E 2Z7

GARDEN CLUBS OF ONTARIO
8 Tanager Avenue
Toronto, Ontario M4G 3R1

MANITOBA HORTICULTURAL ASSOCIATON
908 Norquay Boulevard
Winnipeg, Manitoba
R3C 0P8

NEW BRUNSWICK HORTICULTURAL SOCIETY
Department of Agriculture
Horticulture Section
Box 6000
Fredericton, New Brunswick
E3B 5H1

SUPPLIERS OF
WILD-GARDEN MATERIALS

NEWFOUNDLAND
HORTICULTURAL SOCIETY
Box 4326
St. Johns, Newfoundland
A1C 6C4

NORTH AMERICAN HEATHER
SOCIETY
1205 Copley Place
R.R. 1
Shawigan Lake, British
Columbia   V0R 2W0

NOVA SCOTIA ASSOCIATION
OF GARDEN CLUBS
Box 550
Truro, Nova Scotia B2N 5E3

ONTARIO HORTICULTURAL
ASSOCIATION
Ontario Ministry of Agriculture
and Food
Rural Organizations Service
Branch
Box 1030
Guelph, Ontario N1H 6N1

PRINCE EDWARD ISLAND
RURAL BEAUTIFICATION
SOCIETY
Box 1194
Charlottetown,
Prince Edward Island
C1A 7M8

ROYAL BOTANICAL GARDENS
MEMBERS ASSOCIATION
Box 339
Hamilton, Ontario L8N 3H8

SASKATCHEWAN
HORTICULTURAL
ASSOCIATION
Box 152
Balcarres, Saskatchewan
S0G 0C0

LA SOCIÉTÉ D'ANIMATION
DU JARDIN ET DE L'INSTITUT
BOTANIQUES
4101 rue Sherbrooke est
Montréal, Québec H1X 2B2

United States

APPLEWOOD SEED COMPANY
5380 Vivian Street
Arvada, CO 80002

THE BOVEES NURSERY
1737 S.W. Coronado
Portland, OR 97219

CLYDE ROBIN SEED CO.
Box 2855
Castro Valley, CA 94546

ENVIRONMENTAL SEED
PRODUCERS, INC.
PO Box 5904
El Monte, CA 91734

GARDENS OF THE BLUE RIDGE
P.O. Box 10
Pineola, NC 28662

U.S. DEPARTMENT OF
AGRICULTURE
LOCAL OFFICE OF THE SOIL
CONSERVATION SERVICE
(Look in phone book under
"FEDERAL." Or contact your
County Extension Agent.)

VICK'S WILDGARDENS
Box 115
Gladwyne, PA 19035

Canada

ALBERTA NURSERIES & SEEDS,
LTD.
Box 20
Bowden, Alberta
T0M 0K0

ALPENGLOW GARDENS
13328 King George Highway
North Surrey, British Columbia
V3T 2T6

ATLANTIC PROVINCES
NURSERY TRADES
ASSOCIATION
130 Bluewater Road
Bedford, Nova Scotia
B4A 1G7

BEAVERLODGE NURSERY, LTD.
Box 127
Beaverlodge, Alberta T0H 0C0

BRITISH COLUMBIA NURSERY
TRADES ASSOCIATION
Suite #101-A-15290-103A
Avenue
Surrey, British Columbia
V3R 7A2

CANADIAN NURSERY
TRADES ASSOCIATION
1293 Matheson Boulevard
Mississauga, Ontario L4W 1R1

CANADIAN SEED GROWERS
ASSOCIATION
237 Argyle Avenue
Box 8455
Ottawa, Ontario   K1G 3T1

DOWNHAM NURSERY, INC.
626 Victoria Street
Strathroy, Ontario N7G 3C1

FLOWERS CANADA
115 Suffolk Street West
Guelph, Ontario N1H 2J7

GARDENERS AND FLORISTS
ASSOCIATION OF ONTARIO
540 The West Mall No. 5
Etobicoke, Ontario M9C 1G3

GREENHEDGES
650 Montée de Liesse
Montréal, Québec
H4T 1N8

JOHN CONNON NURSERIES
Waterdown, Ontario
L0R 2H0

MANITOBA NURSERY &
LANDSCAPE ASSOCIATION
104 Parkside Drive
Winnipeg, Manitoba
R3J 3P8

McCONNELL NURSERIES
R.R. 1
Port Burwell, Ontario
N0J 1T0

NURSERY SOD GROWERS'
ASSOCIATION OF ONTARIO
Carlisle, Ontario
L0R 1H0

SASKATCHEWAN NURSERY
TRADES ASSOCIATION
Box 460
Carnduff, Saskatchewan
S0C 0S0

SHERIDAN NURSERIES
1116 Winston Churchill
Boulevard
Oakville, Ontario
L6J 4Z2

WILLIAM DAM SEEDS
Highway 8
West Flamborough, Ontario
L0R 2K0

WOODLAND NURSERIES
2151 Camilla Road
Mississauga, Ontario
L5A 2K1

REGIONAL WILD-FLOWER MIXES

Dry Mixture (grows in regions with 10–30 inches rainfall/year)

SCIENTIFIC NAME	COMMON NAME	TYPE*	COLOR
Achillea millefolium	White Yarrow	P	White
Centaurea cyanus	Cornflower	A	Blue
Chrysanthemum carinatum	Painted Daisy	A	White/Yellow/Red/Purple
Coreopsis tinctoria	Plains Coreopsis	A	Yellow/Maroon
Dianthus barbatus/D. deltoides	Pinks (Sweet William; Maiden)	P	Pink/Red/White
Eschscholzia californica	California Poppy	TP	Yellow/Orange
Gaillardia aristata	Perennial Gaillardia	P	Yellow/Red
Gaillardia pulchella	Annual Gaillardia	A	Yellow/Red
Gyposophila elegans	Baby's Breath	A	White
Linaria maroccana	Spurred Snapdragon	A	Pink/Yellow/Violet
Linum perenne lewisii	Blue Flax	P	Blue
Lobularia maritima	Sweet Alyssum	TP	White
Oenothera missouroensis	Dwarf Evening Primrose	P	Yellow
Papaver rhoeas	Corn Poppy	A	White/Pink/Red
Penstemon strictus	Penstemon	P	Blue
Ratibida columnifera	Prairie Coneflower	B/P	Yellow/Red
Silene armeria	Catchfly	A/B	Pink

Moist Mixture (over 30 inches rainfall/year)

SCIENTIFIC NAME	COMMON NAME	TYPE*	COLOR
Aquilegia caerulea/A. vulgaris	Columbine	P	Yellow/Red/Violet/Blue
Cheiranthus allionii/C. cheiri	Wallflower	P	Orange/Pink/Red
Crysanthemum leucanthemum	Ox-Eye Daisy	P	White
Clarkia unguiculata	Clarkia	A	Pink/Lavender
Coreopsis lanceolata	Lance-Leaved Coreopsis	P	Yellow
Delphinium ajacis	Rocket Larkspur	A	White/Pink/Blue/Violet
Echinacea purpurea	Purple Coneflower	P	Purple
Hesperis matronalis	Dame's Rocket	P	Violet
Iberis umbellata	Candytuft	A	White/Pink/Violet
Lavatera trimestris	Tree Mallow	A	White/Pink/Violet
Liatris spicata	Gayfeather	P	Purple
Linum grandiflorium rubrum	Scarlet Flax	A	Scarlet
Myosotis sylvatica	Forget-Me-Not	A	Blue
Nemophila menziesii	Baby Blue-Eyes	A	Blue
Rudbeckia hirta	Black-Eyed Susan	A/B/P	Yellow
Viola cornuta	Johnny Jump-up	P	Purple/Yellow/Blue

*A = Annual; B = Biennial; P = Perennial; TP = Tender perennial, grown as an annual in cold climates.

Knee-Hi Mixture (less than 24 inches high)

SCIENTIFIC NAME	COMMON NAME	TYPE*	COLOR
Centaurea cyanus (dwarf)	Dwarf Cornflower	A	Blue
Cheiranthus allionii	Wallflower	B/P	Orange
Coreopsis lanceolata	Lance-Leaved Coreopsis	P	Yellow
Coreopsis tinctoria	Plains Coreopsis	A/B	Yellow/Maroon
Delphinium ajacis	Rocket Larkspur	A	White/Pink/Blue/Violet
Dimorphotheca aurantiaca	African Daisy	A	White/Orange/Salmon
Eschscholzia californica	California Poppy	TP	Yellow/Orange
Gaillardia aristata	Perennial Gaillardia	P	Yellow/Red
Gypsophila elegans	Baby's Breath	A	White
Iberis grandiflorium rubrum	Scarlet Flax	A	Scarlet
Linum perenne lewisii	Blue Flax	P	Blue
Lobularia maritima	Sweet Alyssum	TP	White
Papaver rhoeas	Corn Poppy	A	White/Pink/Red
Ratibida columnifera	Prairie Coneflower	B/P	Yellow/Red
Rudbeckia hirta	Black-Eyed Susan	A/B/P	Yellow
Silene armeria	Catchfly	A/B	Pink

Low-Growing Mixture (less than 16 inches high)

SCIENTIFIC NAME	COMMON NAME	TYPE*	COLOR
Centaurea cyanus (dwarf)	Dwarf Cornflower	A	Blue
Cheiranthus allionii	Wallflower	B/P	Orange
Coreopsis lanceolata (dwarf)	Dwarf Lance-Leaved Coreopsis	P	Yellow
Coreopsis tinctoria (dwarf)	Dwarf Plains Coreopsis	A	Yellow/Maroon
Dimorphotheca aurantiaca	African Daisy	A	White/Orange/Salmon
Eschscholzia californica	California Poppy	TP	Yellow/Orange
Gypsophila elegans	Baby's Breath	A	White
Iberis umbellata	Candytuft	A	White/Pink/Violet
Linaria maroccana	Spurred Snapdragon	A	Pink/Yellow/Violet
Lobularia maritima	Sweet Alyssum	TP	White
Myosotis sylvatica	Forget-Me-Not	A	Blue
Oenothera missouriensis	Dwarf Evening Primrose	P	Yellow
Papaver nudicaule	Iceland Poppy	P	White/Yellow/Orange
Phacelia campanularia	California Bluebell	A	Blue
Silene armeria (dwarf)	Dwarf Catchfly	A	Pink
Viola cornuta	Johnny Jump-up	P	Purple/Yellow/Blue

*A = Annual; B = Biennial; P = Perennial; TP = Tender perennial, grown as an annual in cold climates.

Shade Mixture

SCIENTIFIC NAME	COMMON NAME	TYPE*	COLOR
Aquilegia caerulea/A. vulgaris	Columbine	P	Yellow/Red/Violet/Blue
Chrysanthemum leucanthemum	Ox-Eye Daisy	P	White
Clarkia unguiculata	Clarkia	A	Pink/Lavender
Coreopsis lanceolata	Lance-Leaved Coreopsis	P	Yellow
Delphinium ajacis	Rocket Larkspur	A	White/Pink/Blue/Violet
Dianthus barbatus	Sweet William Pink	P	Red
Echinacea purpurea	Purple Coneflower	P	Purple
Gypsophila elegans	Baby's Breath	A	White
Hesperis matronalis	Dame's Rocket	P	Violet
Iberis umbellata	Candytuft	A	White/Pink/Violet
Linaria maroccana	Spurred Snapdragon	A	Pink/Yellow/Violet
Mimulus tigrinus	Monkeyflower	A	Yellow/Red
Myosotis sylvatica	Forget-Me-Not	A/B	Blue
Nemophila menziesii	Baby Blue-Eyes	A	Blue
Papaver rhoeas	Corn Poppy	A	White/Pink/Red
Viola cornuta	Johnny Jump-up	P	Purple/Yellow/Blue

Fast-Growing Species

SCIENTIFIC NAME	COMMON NAME	TYPE*	COLOR
Achillea millefolium	White Yarrow	P	White
Centaurea cyanus	Cornflower	A	Blue
Cerastium biebersteinii	Snow-in-Summer	P	White
Cheiranthus allionii	Wallflower	B/P	Orange
Cheiranthus cheiri	Wallflower	B/P	Orange/Pink/Violet
Cichorium intybus	Chicory	P	Blue
Cosmos bipinnatus	Cosmos	A	White/Pink/Crimson
Eschscholzia californica	California Poppy	TP	Yellow/Orange
Gypsophila elegans	Annual Baby's Breath	A	White
Gypsophila paniculata	Perennial Baby's Breath	P	White
Helianthus annuus	Sunflower	A	Yellow
Hesperis matronalis	Dame's Rocket	P	Violet
Lathyrus latifolius	Perennial Sweet Pea	P	Rose/Pink
Linum perenne lewisii	Blue Flax	P	Blue
Lotus corniculatus	Bird's-Foot Trefoil	P	Yellow
Oenothera hooken	Tall Evening Primrose	B/P	Yellow
Rudbeckia hirta	Black-Eyed Susan	A/B/P	Yellow
Sanguisorba minor	Small Burnet	P	Green

*A = Annual; B = Biennial; P = Perennial; TP = Tender perennial, grown as an annual in cold climates.

Midwest Mixture

SCIENTIFIC NAME	COMMON NAME	TYPE*	COLOR
Achillea fipendulina	Gold Yarrow	P	Gold
Achillea millefolium	White Yarrow	P	White
Aquilegia caerulea	Columbine	P	Yellow/Red/Violet/Blue
Campanula rotundi-folia/C. carpatica	Harebell/Bellflower	P	Lavender/Blue
Centaurea cyanus	Cornflower	A	Blue
Cerastium biebersteinii	Snow-in-Summer	P	White
Cheiranthus allionii/C. cheiri	Wallflower	B/P	Orange/Pink/Red
Chrysanthemum leucanthemum	Ox-Eye Daisy	P	White
Delphinium ajacis	Rocket Larkspur	A	White/Pink/Blue/Violet
Dianthus barbatus/D. deltoides	Pinks (Sweet William; Maiden)	P	Pink/Red/White
Eschscholzia californica	California Poppy	TP	Yellow/Orange
Gaillardia aristata	Perennial Gaillardia	P	Yellow/Red
Gyposophila elegans	Baby's Breath	A	White
Hesperis matronalis	Dame's Rocket	P	Violet
Linum perenne lewisii	Blue Flax	P	Blue
Lupinus perennis	Perennial Lupine	P	Blue
Myosotis sylvatica	Forget-Me-Not	A/B	Blue
Oenothera missouriensis	Dwarf Evening Primrose	P	Yellow
Penstemon strictus	Penstemon	P	Blue
Rudbeckia hirta	Black-Eyed Susan	A/B/P	Yellow
Silene armeria	Catchfly	A/B	Pink

Northeast Mixture

SCIENTIFIC NAME	COMMON NAME	TYPE*	COLOR
Achillea fipendulina	Gold Yarrow	P	Gold
Achillea millefolium	White Yarrow	P	White
Aster novae-angliae	New England Aster	P	Violet
Centaurea cyanus	Cornflower	A	Blue
Cheiranthus allionii/C. cheiri	Wallflower	B/P	Orange/Pink/Red
Chrysanthemum leucanthemum	Ox-Eye Daisy	P	White
Coreopsis lanceolata	Lance-Leaved Coreopsis	P	Yellow
Delphinium ajacis	Rocket Larkspur	A	White/Pink/Blue/Violet
Dianthus barbatus/D. deltoides	Pinks (Sweet William; Maiden)	P	Pink/Red/White
Digitalis purpurea	Foxglove	B/P	Purple/Cream
Echinacea purpurea	Purple Coneflower	P	Purple
Gypsophila elegans	Baby's Breath	A	White
Hesperis matronalis	Dame's Rocket	P	Violet

*A = Annual; B = Biennial; P = Perennial; TP = Tender perennial, grown as an annual in cold climates.

Ipomopsis rubra	Gilia	B	White/Red/Coral
Liatris spicata	Gayfeather	P	Purple
Linaria maroccana	Spurred Snapdragon	A	Pink/Yellow/Violet
Linum grandiflorium rubrum	Scarlet Flax	A	Scarlet
Lupinus perennis	Perennial Lupine	P	Blue
Oenothera missouriensis	Dwarf Evening Primrose	P	Yellow
Papaver rhoeas	Corn Poppy	A	White/Pink/Red
Rudbeckia hirta	Black-Eyed Susan	A/B/P	Yellow
Silene armeria	Catchfly	A/B	Pink

Northwest Mixture (grows below an altitude of 7,000 feet)

SCIENTIFIC NAME	COMMON NAME	TYPE*	COLOR
Aquilegia caerulea	Columbine	P	Yellow/Red/Violet/Blue
Cheirianthus allionii/C. cheiri	Wallflower	B/P	Orange/Pink/Red
Chrysanthemum leucanthemum	Ox-Eye Daisy	P	White
Clarkia unguiculata	Clarkia	A	Pink/Lavender
Collinsia heterphylla	Chinese House	A	White/Violet
Coreopsis lanceolata	Lance-Leaved Coreopsis	P	Yellow
Delphinium ajacis	Rocket Larkspur	A	White/Pink/Blue/Violet
Dianthus barbatus/D. deltoides	Pinks (Sweet William; Maiden)	P	Pink/Red/White
Eschscholzia californica	California Poppy	TP	Yellow/Orange
Gilia tricolor	Bird's-Eye	A	Lavender/White
Hesperis matronalis	Dame's Rocket	P	Violet
Liatris spicata	Gayfeather	P	Purple
Linaria maroccana	Spurred Snapdragon	A	Pink/Yellow/Violet
Linum grandiflorium rubrum	Scarlet Flax	A	Scarlet
Lobularia maritima	Sweet Alyssum	TP	White
Mirabilis jalapa	Four-O'Clock	TP	Red/Pink/Yellow/White
Nemophila maculata	Five-Spot	A	White/Purple
Nemophila menziesii	Baby Blue-Eyes	A	Blue
Papaver rhoeas	Corn Poppy	A	White/Pink/Red
Rudbeckia hirta	Black-Eyed Susan	A/B/P	Yellow
Silene armeria	Catchfly	A/B	Pink

Southeast Mixture

SCIENTIFIC NAME	COMMON NAME	TYPE*	COLOR
Centaurea cyanus	Cornflower	A	Blue
Cheiranthus allionii/C. cheiri	Wallflower	B/P	Orange/Pink/Red
Coreopsis lanceolata	Lance-Leaved Coreopsis	P	Yellow

*A = Annual; B = Biennial; P = Perennial; TP = Tender perennial, grown as an annual in cold climates.

Coreopsis tinctoria	Plains Coreopsis	A	Yellow/Maroon
Delphinium ajacis	Rocket Larkspur	A	White/Pink/Blue/Violet
Echinacea purpurea	Purple Coneflower	P	Purple
Eschscholzia californica	California Poppy	TP	Yellow/Orange
Gaillardia pulchella	Annual Gaillardia	A	Yellow/Red
Gilia tricolor	Bird's-Eye	A	Lavender/White
Gypsophila elegans	Baby's Breath	A	White
Hesperis matronalis	Dame's Rocket	P	Violet
Ipomopsis rubra	Gilia	B	White/Red/Coral
Lavatera trimestris	Tree Mallow	A	White/Pink/Violet
Liatris spicata	Gayfeather	P	Purple
Linum grandiflorium rubrum	Scarlet Flax	A	Scarlet
Lobularia maritima	Sweet Alyssum	TP	White
Lupinus perennis	Perennial Lupine	P	Blue
Mirabilis jalapa	Four-O'Clock	YP	Red/Pink/Yellow/White
Nemophila menziesii	Baby Blue-Eyes	A	Blue
Papaver rhoeas	Corn Poppy	A	White/Pink/Red
Rudbeckia hirta	Black-Eyed Susan	A/B/P	Yellow

Southwest Mixture (grows below an altitude of 7,000 feet)

SCIENTIFIC NAME	COMMON NAME	TYPE*	COLOR
Achillea filipendulina	Gold Yarrow	P	Gold
Achillea millefolium	White Yarrow	P	White
Centaurea cyanus	Cornflower	A	Blue
Clarkia unguiculata	Clarkia	A	Pink/Lavender
Coreopsis tinctoria	Plains Coreopsis	A	Yellow/Maroon
Dimorphotheca africana	African Daisy	A	White/Orange/Salmon
Eschscholzia californica	California Poppy	TP	Yellow/Orange
Gaillardia pulchella	Annual Gaillardia	A	Yellow/Red
Cheiranthus allionii/C. cheiri	Wallflower	B/P	Orange/Pink/Red
Chrysanthemum carinatum	Painted Daisy	A	White/Yellow/Red/Purple
Coreopsis lanceolata	Lance-Leaved Coreopsis	P	Yellow
Coreopsis tinctoria	Plains Coreopsis	A	Yellow/Maroon
Dianthus barbatus/D. deltoides	Pinks (Sweet William; Maiden)	P	Pink/Red/White
Dimorphotheca aurantiaca	African Daisy	A	White/Orange/Salmon
Echinacea purpurea	Purple Coneflower	P	Purple
Gaillardia aristata	Perennial Gaillardia	P	Yellow/Red
Gaillardia pulchella	Annual Gaillardia	A	Yellow/Red
Gypsophila elegans	Baby's Breath	A	White
Iberis umbellata	Candytuft	A	White/Pink/Violet
Linum grandiflorium rubrum	Scarlet Flax	A	Scarlet

*A = Annual; B = Biennial; P = Perennial; TP = Tender perennial, grown as an annual in cold climates.

Linum perenne lewisii	Blue Flax	P	Blue
Lobularia maritima	Sweet Alyssum	TP	White
Lupinus texensis	Texas Bluebonnet	A	Blue
Mirabilis jalapa	Four-O'Clock	TP	Red/Pink/Yellow/White
Nemophila menziesii	Baby Blue-Eyes	A	Blue
Gilia tricolor	Bird's-Eye	A	Lavender/White
Gypsophila elegans	Baby's Breath	A	White
Layia platyglossa	Tidy-Tips	A	Yellow/White
Linaria maroccana	Spurred Snapdragon	A	Pink/Yellow/Violet
Linum grandiflorum	Scarlet Flax	A	Scarlet
Linum perenne lewisii	Blue Flax	P	Blue
Lobularia maritima	Sweet Alyssum	TP	White
Machaeranthera tanacetifolia	Prairie Aster	B	Violet
Mirabilis jalapa	Four-O'Clock	TP	Red/Pink/Yellow/White
Nemophila maculata	Five-Spot	A	White/Purple
Nemophila menziesii	Baby Blue-Eyes	A	Blue
Papaver rhoeas	Corn Poppy	A	White/Pink/Red
Penstemon spp.	Penstemon	P	Lavender/Blue/Purple
Ratibida columnifera	Prairie Coneflower	B/P	Yellow/Red

Texas/Oklahoma Mixture

SCIENTIFIC NAME	COMMON NAME	TYPE*	COLOR
Achillea filipendulina	Gold Yarrow	P	Gold
Achillea millefolium	White Yarrow	P	White
Centaurea cyanus	Cornflower	A	Blue
Oenothera missouriensis	Dwarf Evening Primrose	P	Yellow
Papaver rhoeas	Corn Poppy	A	White/Pink/Red
Ratibida columnifera	Prairie Coneflower	B/P	Yellow/Red
Rudbeckia hirta	Black-Eyed Susan	A/B/P	Yellow

Western Mixture (grows below an altitude of 7,000 feet)

SCIENTIFIC NAME	COMMON NAME	TYPE*	COLOR
Achillea filipendulina	Gold Yarrow	P	Gold
Achillea millefolium	White Yarrow	P	White
Centaurea cyanus	Cornflower	A	Blue
Cerastium biebersteinii	Snow-in-Summer	P	White
Chrysanthemum carinatum	Painted Daisy	A	Yellow/Red/Purple/White
Clarkia unguiculata	Clarkia	A	Pink/Lavender
Coreopsis tinctoria	Plains Coreopsis	A	Yellow/Maroon

*A = Annual; B = Biennial; P = Perennial; TP = Tender perennial, grown as an annual in cold climates.

Dianthus barbatus/D. deltoides	Pinks (Sweet William; Maiden)	P	Pink/Red/White
Dimorphotheca aurantiaca	African Daisy	A	White/Orange/Salmon
Eschscholzia californica	California Poppy	TP	Yellow/Orange
Gaillardia aristata	Perennial Gaillardia	P	Yellow/Red
Gaillardia pulchella	Annual Gaillardia	A	Yellow/Red
Gypsophila elegans	Baby's Breath	A	White
Iberis umbellata	Candytuft	A	White/Pink/Violet
Linaria maroccana	Spurred Snapdragon	A	Pink/Yellow/Violet
Linum grandiflorium rubrum	Scarlet Flax	A	Scarlet
Linum perenne lewisii	Blue Flax	P	Blue
Lobularia maritima	Sweet Alyssum	TP	White
Lupinus perennis	Perennial Lupine	P	Blue
Machaeranthera tanacetifolia	Prairie Aster	B	Violet
Oenothera missouriensis	Dwarf Evening Primrose	P	Yellow
Papaver rhoeas	Corn Poppy	A	White/Pink/Red
Penstemon strictus	Penstemon	P	Blue
Ratibida columnifera	Prairie Coneflower	B/P	Yellow/Red

Gulf Coast/Caribbean Mixture (includes southern Texas and southern Florida)

SCIENTIFIC NAME	COMMON NAME	TYPE*	COLOR
Asparagus densiflorus sprengen	Asparagus sprengen	TP	White
Centaurea cyanus	Cornflower	A	Blue
Cheiranthus allionii/C. cheiri	Wallflower	B/P	Orange/Pink/Red
Coreopsis lanceolata	Lance-Leaved Coreopsis	P	Yellow
Cosmos bipinnatus	Cosmos	A	White/Pink/Crimson
Dimorphotheca aurantiaca	African Daisy	A	White/Orange/Salmon
Gaillardia pulchella	Annual Gaillardia	A	Yellow/Red
Gypsophila elegans	Baby's Breath	A	White
Liatris spicata	Gayfeather	P	Purple
Linaria maroccana	Spurred Snapdragon	A	Pink/Yellow/Violet
Linum grandiflorium rubrum	Scarlet Flax	A	Scarlet
Linum perenne lewisii	Blue Flax	P	Blue
Lobularia maritima	Sweet Alyssum	TP	White
Mirabilis jalapa	Four-O'Clock	TP	Red/Pink/Yellow/White
Rudbeckia hirta	Black-Eyed Susan	A/B/P	Yellow
Silene armeria	Catchfly	A/B	Pink
Thunbergia alata	Black-Eyed Susan Vine	TP	Yellow-Orange

*A = Annual; B = Biennial; P = Perennial; TP = Tender perennial, grown as an annual in cold climates.

INDIVIDUAL WILD-FLOWER SPECIES LIST

SN = SCIENTIFIC NAME
CN = COMMON NAME
T = TYPE
    A = Annual
    B = Biennial
    P = Perennial
    TP = Tender perennial, grown as an
        annual in cold climates
	CR = CULTURAL REQUIREMENTS
	    Sun/Shade = Full sun or shade
	    P/Sun = Full or partial sun
	    P/Shade = Partial sun or shade
	    Dry = 10–30 inches rainfall per year, or
	        sandy, well-drained soil
	    Moist = Over 30 inches rainfall per year,
	        or regular irrigation
		MH = MAXIMUM HEIGHT (IN INCHES)
		C = COLOR
		BP = BLOOM PERIOD
		    Sp = Spring
		    S = Summer
		    F = Fall
		S/L = SEEDS PER LB.
		MG = MINIMUM GERMINATION %

SN –*Achillea filipendulina*
CN –Gold Yarrow
T –P
CR –Sun/Dry/Moist
MH –60
C –Gold
BP –S
S/L –3,200,000
MG –50

SN –*Achillea millefolium*
CN –White Yarrow
T –P
CR –Sun/Dry/Moist
MH –36
C –White
BP –S
S/L –3,200,000
MG –50

SN –*Achillea millefolium rubrum*
CN –Red Yarrow
T –P
CR –Sun/Dry/Moist
MH –24
C –Red
BP –S
S/L –3,200,000
MG –50

SN –*Anagallis arvensis*
CN –Pimpernel
T –A
CR –P/Sun/Moist/Dry
MH –10
C –Scarlet/Pink/Salmon/Blue
BP –S
S/L –544,000
MG –60

SN –*Aquilegia caerulea*
CN –Columbine
T –A
CR –Sun/Shade/Moist
MH –36
C –Yellow/Red/Violet/Blue
BP –Sp/S
S/L –365,000
MG –50

SN –*Aquilegia vulgaris*
CN –Dwarf Columbine
T –P
CR –P/Shade/Moist
MH –18
C –Red/Violet/Blue
BP –Sp/S
S/L –368,000
MG –50

SN –*Arabis alpina, A. Caucasica*
CN –Rockcress
T –P
CR –P/Sun/Dry
MH –12
BP –Sp/S
S/L –2,400,000
MG –60

SN –*Asparagus densiflorus sprengen*
CN –Asparagus sprengen
T –P
CR –P/Sun/Moist
MH –24
C –White
BP –S
S/L –11,200
MG –55

SN –*Aster novae-angliae*
CN –New England Aster
T –P
CR –Sun/Shade/Dry/Moist
MH –72
C –Violet
BP –F
S/L –1,216,000
MG –40

SN –*Campanula carpatica*
CN –Tussock Bellflower
T –P
CR –Sun/Shade/Dry/Moist
MH –12
C –Lavender/Blue
BP –S
S/L –4,528,000
MG –50

SN –*Campanula rotundifolia*
CN –Scotch Harebell
T –P
CR –Sun/Shade/Dry/Moist
MH –12
C –Lavender/Blue
BP –S
S/L –4,528,000
MG –50

SN –*Castilleia spp.*
CN –Indian Paintbrush
T –P
CR –P/Sun/Dry/Moist
MH –24
C –Scarlet
BP –S/F
S/L –4,000,000
MG –50

SN –*Centaurea cyanus*
CN –Cornflower
T –A
CR –P/Sun/Dry
MH –30
C –Blue
BP –S
S/L –96,000
MG –60

SN –*Centaurea cyanus (dwarf)*
CN –Dwarf Cornflower
T –A
CR –P/Sun/Dry
MH –12
C –Blue
BP –S
S/L –96,000
MG –60

SN –*Ceratum biebersteinii*
CN –Snow-in-Summer
T –P
CR –P/Sun/Dry/Moist
MH –12
C –White
BP –Sp/S
S/L –1,300,000
MG –70

SN –*Cheiranthus allionii*
CN –Wallflower
T –B/P
CR –P/Sun/Dry/Moist
MH–18
C –Orange
BP –S
S/L –340,000
MG–65

SN –*Cheiranthus cheiri*
CN –Wallflower
T –B/P
CR –P/Sun/Dry/Moist
MH–24
C –Orange/Pink/Red
BP –Sp
S/L –304,000
MG–65

SN –*Chrysanthemum carinatum*
CN –Painted Daisy
T –A
CR –P/Sun/Dry/Moist
MH–36
C –White/Yellow/Red/Purple
BP –S/F
S/L –159,000
MG–40

SN –*Chrysanthemum leucanthemum*
CN –Ox-Eye Daisy
T –P
CR –P/Sun/Moist
MH–24
C –White
BP –S
S/L –400,000
MG–65

SN –*Chrysanthemum leucanthemum* (dwarf)
CN –Dwarf Ox-Eye Daisy
T –P
CR –P/Sun/Moist
MH–16
C –White
BP –S
S/L –400,000
MG–65

SN –*Chicorium intybus*
CN –Chicory
T –P
CR –P/Sun/Dry
MH–60
C –Blue
BP –S/F
S/L –425,000
MG–65

SN –*Clarkia unguiculata*
CN –Clarkia
T –A
CR –Sun/Dry/Moist
MH–30
C –Pink/Lavender
BP –Sp/S
S/L –1,580,000
MG–65

SN –*Collinsia heterophylla*
CN –Chinese House
T –A
MH–24
C –White/Violet
BP –Sp/S
S/L –408,000
MG–50

SN –*Coreopsis lanceolata*
CN –Lance-leaved Coreopsis
T –P
CR –P/Sun/Dry/Moist
MH–24
C –Yellow
BP –S/F
S/L –221,000
MG–40

SN –*Coreopsis lanceolata* (dwarf)
CN –Dwarf Lance-leaved Coreopsis
T –P
CR –P/Sun/Dry/Moist
MH–16
C –Yellow
BP –S/F
S/L –221,000
MG–40

SN –*Coreopsis tintoria*
CN –Dwarf Plains Coreopsis
T –A
CR –P/Sun/Dry/Moist
MH–18
C –Yellow/Maroon
BP –S/F
S/L –1,400,000
MG–65

SN –*Cosmos bipinnatus*
CN –Cosmos
T –A
CR –P/Sun/Dry
MH–60
C –White/Pink/Crimson
BP –S/F
S/L –80,000
MG–65

SN –*Delphinium ajacis*
CN –Rocket Larkspur
T –A
CR –P/Sun/Moist
MH–24
C –White/Pink/Blue/Violet
BP –S
S/L –150,000
MG–50

SN –*Dianthus barbatus*
CN –Sweet William Pink
T –P
CR –P/Shade/Moist
MH–18
C –White/Pink/Red
BP –S
S/L –150,000
MG–60

SN –*Dianthus deltoides*
CN –Maiden Pink
T –P
CR –Sun/Dry/Moist
MH–18
C –Pink
BP –S
S/L –2,480,000
MG–60

SN –*Dicentra eximia*
CN –Bleeding Heart
T –P
CR –P/Shade/Moist
MH–24
C –Pink
BP –Sp
S/L –208,000
MG–50

SN –*Digitalis purpurea*
CN –Foxglove
T –P
CR –P/Shade/Moist
MH–48
C –Purple/Cream
BP –S
S/L –4,490,000
MG–60

SN –*Dimorphetheca aurantiaca*
CN –African Daisy
T –A
CR –Sun/Dry
MH–12
C –Orange/Salmon/White
BP –S/F
S/L –225,000
MG–55

SN = SCIENTIFIC NAME
CN = COMMON NAME
T = TYPE
    A = Annual
    B = Biennial
    P = Perennial
    TP = Tender perennial, grown as an
             annual in cold climates

CR = CULTURAL REQUIREMENTS
    Sun/Shade = Full sun or shade
    P/Sun = Full or partial sun
    P/Shade = Partial sun or shade
    Dry = 10–30 inches rainfall per year, or
           sandy, well-drained soil
    Moist = Over 30 inches rainfall per year,
           or regular irrigation

MH = MAXIMUM HEIGHT (IN INCHES)
C = COLOR
BP = BLOOM PERIOD
    Sp = Spring
    S = Summer
    F = Fall
S/L = SEEDS PER LB.
MG = MINIMUM GERMINATION %

SN –*Echinacea purpurea*
CN –Purple Coneflower
T –P
CR –P/Shade/Dry/Moist
MH –36
C –Purple
BP –S
S/L –117,000
MG –60

SN –*Erigeron speciosus*
CN –Fleabane Daisy
T –P
CR –P/Sun/Dry/Moist
MH –24
C –Violet
BP –Sp/S
S/L –1,600,000
MG –60

SN –*Eschscholzia californica*
CN –California Poppy
T –TP
CR –Sun/Dry
MH –18
C –Yellow/Orange
BP –Sp/S
S/L –290,000
MG –60

SN –*Gaillardia aristata*
CN –Perennial Gaillardia
T –A
CR –Sun/Dry
MH –24
C –Yellow/Red
BP –S
S/L –132,000
MG –45

SN –*Gaillardia pulchella*
CN –Annual Gaillardia
T –A
CR –Sun/Dry
C –Yellow/Red
BP –S
S/L –153,000
MG –45

SN –*Gilia tricolor*
CN –Bird's-Eye
T –A
CR –Sun/Dry
MH –12
C –Lavender/White
BP –Sp
S/L –1,100,000
MG –65

SN –*Gypsophilia elegans*
CN –Baby's Breath
T –A
CR –P/Sun/Dry
MH –18
C –White
BP –S
S/L –174,000
MG –70

SN –*Gypsophilia panculata*
CN –Perennial Baby's Breath
T –P
CR –Sun/Dry/Moist
C –White
BP –S
S/L –512,000
MG –70

SN –*Helianthus annuus*
CN –Sunflower
T –A
CR –Sun/Dry
MH –72
C –Yellow
BP –S
S/L –58,000
MG –65

SN –*Hesperis matronalis*
CN –Dame's Rocket
T –P
CR –P/Shade/Moist
MH –36
C –Violet
BP –Sp/S
S/L –296,000
MG –65

SN –*Iberis umbellata*
CN –Candytuft
T –A
CR –P/Sun/Dry/Moist
MH –16
C –White/Pink/Violet
BP –S
S/L –103,000
MG –65

SN –*Ipomopsis rubra*
CN –Gilia
T –B
CR –P/Sun/Dry/Moist
MH –72
C –Red/White/Coral
BP –S
S/L –341,000
MG –65

SN –*Lathyrus latifolius*
CN –Perennial Sweet Pea
T –P
CR –P/Sun/Dry/Moist
C –Rose/Pink
BP –S
S/L –9,000
MG –75

SN –*Lavatera trimestris*
CN –Tree Mallow
T –A
CR –Sun/Moist
MH –36
C –White/Pink/Violet
BP –S/F
S/L –68,000
MG –50

SN –*Layia platyglossa*
CN –Tidy-Tips
T –A
CR –P/Sun/Dry
MH –12
C –Yellow/White
BP –S
S/L –323,000
MG –50

SN –*Liatris spicata*
CN –Gayfeather
T –P
CR –P/Sun-Moist
MH –48
C –Purple
BP –S/F
S/L –136,000
MG –50

SN –*Linaria moroccana*
CN –Spurred Snapdragon
T –A
CR –P/Sun/Dry
MH –16
C –Pink/Yellow/Violet
BP –Sp/S
S/L –122,000
MG –60

SN –*Linum grandiflorium rubrum*
CN –Scarlet Flax
T –A
CR –P/Sun/Dry/Moist
MH –18
C –Scarlet
BP –S
S/L –122,000
MG –60

SN –*Linum perenne lewisii*
CN –Blue Flax
T –P
CR –Sun/Dry/Moist
MH –24
C –Blue
BP –Sp/S
S/L –293,000
MG –60

SN –*Lobularia maritima*
CN –Sweet Alyssum
T –TP
CR –P/Sun/Dry/Moist
MH –12
C –White
BP –Sp
S/L –1,250,000
MG –60

SN –*Lotus corniculatus*
CN –Birds Foot Treefoil
T –P
CR –Sun/Moist
MH –24
C –Yellow
BP –S
S/L –418,000
MG –50

SN –*Lupinus perennis*
CN –Perrenial Lupine
T –P
CR –Sun/Dry/Moist
MH –12
C –Blue
BP –Sp/S
S/L –22,000
MG –65

SN –*Lupinus texensis*
CN –Texas Bluebonnet
T –A
CR –P/Sun/Dry
MH –12
C –Blue
BP –Sp
S/L –14,000
MG –65

SN –*Lychnis chalcedonica*
CN –Maltese Cross
T –P
CR –Sun/Dry
MH –24
C –Scarlet/Rose/Salmon
BP –S/F
S/L –225,000
MG –70

SN –*Machaeranthera tanacetifolia*
CN –Prairie Aster
T –B
CR –P/Sun/Dry
MH –18
C –Violet
BP –S/F
S/L –496,000
MG –60

SN –*Minolus spp.*
CN –Monkeyflower
T –A/P
CR –P/Shade/Moist
MH –18
C –Cream/Yellow/Red
BP –Sp/S
S/L –8,800,000
MG –50

SN –*Mirabilis jalapa*
CN –Four O'Clock
T –TP
CR –Sun/Dry/Moist
MH –36
C –Red/Pink/Yellow/White
BP –S/F
S/L –8,000
MG –60

SN –*Myosotis sylvatica*
CN –Forget-Me-Not
T –A/B
CR –P/Shade/Moist
MH –18
C –Blue
BP –Sp
S/L –180,000
MG –50

SN –*Nemophila maculata*
CN –Five-Spot
T –A
CR –P/Shade/Moist
MH –6
C –White/Purple
BP –Sp/S
S/L –82,000
MG –60

SN –*Nemophilia menziesii*
CN –Baby Blue-Eyes
T –A
CR –P/Shade/Moist
MH –12
C –Blue
BP –Sp/S
S/L –260,000
MG –70

SN –*Oenothera hookeri*
CN –Tall Evening Primrose
T –B/P
CR –Sun/Dry/Moist
MH –60
C –Yellow
BP –S
S/L –4,000,000
MG –50

SN –*Oenothera missouriensis*
CN –Dwarf Evening Primrose
T –P
CR –P/Sun/Dry
MH –12
C –Yellow
BP –S
S/L –80,000
MG –50

SN –*Papaver mudicaule*
CN –Iceland Poppy
T –P
CR –Sun/Dry/Moist
MH –15
C –Yellow/Orange/White
BP –Sp/S
S/L –3,200,000
MG –60

SN = SCIENTIFIC NAME	**MH** = MAXIMUM HEIGHT (IN INCHES)
CN = COMMON NAME	**C** = COLOR
T = TYPE	**BP** = BLOOM PERIOD
A = Annual	**Sp** = Spring
B = Biennial	**S** = Summer
P = Perennial	**F** = Fall
TP = Tender perennial, grown as an annual in cold climates	**S/L** = SEEDS PER LB.
	MG = MINIMUM GERMINATION %

CR = CULTURAL REQUIREMENTS
Sun/Shade = Full sun or shade
P/Sun = Full or partial sun
P/Shade = Partial sun or shade
Dry = 10–30 inches rainfall per year, or sandy, well-drained soil
Moist = Over 30 inches rainfall per year, or regular irrigation

---

SN –Papaver rhoeas
CN –Corn Poppy
T –A
CR –P/Sun/Dry
MH–24
C –White/Pink/Red
BP –S
S/L –3,200,000
MG–60

SN –Penstemon strictus
CN –Penstemon
T –P
CR –P/Sun/Dry
MH–24
C –Blue
BP –S
S/L –592,000
MG–60

SN –Penstemon spp.
CN –Penstemon
T –P
CR –P/Sun/Dry
MH–48
C –Purple/Lavender/Blue
BP –S
S/L –500,000
MG–60

SN –Phacelia campanularia
CN –California Bluebell
T –A
CR –Sun/Dry
MH–15
C –Blue
BP –Sp/S
S/L –856,000
MG–65

SN –Phlox drummondii
CN –Annual Phlox
T –A
CR –Sun/Dry
MH–18
C –Rose/White/Red/Lavender/Purple
BP –S/F
S/L –234,000
MG–55

SN –Ratibida columnifera
CN –Prairie Coneflower
T –B/P
CR –P/Sun/Dry
MH–24
C –Yellow/Red
BP –S
S/L –1,230,000
MG–50

SN –Rudbeckia hirta
CN –Black-Eyed Susan
T –A/B/P
CR –P/Sun/Moist
MH–24
C –Yellow
BP –S
S/L –980,000
MG–60

SN –Sanguisorba minor
CN –Small Burnet
T –P
CR –P/Sun/Dry
MH–18
C –Green
BP –Sp/S
S/L –73,000
MG–50

SN –Silene armeria
CN –Catchfly
T –A/B
CR –P/Sun/Dry
MH–16
C –Pink
BP –S
S/L –4,480,000
MG–50

SN –Silene armeria (dwarf)
CN –Dwarf Catchfly
T –A/B
CR –P/Sun/Dry
MH–8
C –Pink
BP –S
S/L –4,480,000
MG–50

SN –Thunbergia alata
CN –Black-Eyed Susan Vine
T –TP
CR –Sun/Moist
MH–22
C –Yellow/Orange
BP –Sp/F
S/L –17,600
MG–60

SN –Thymus serpyllum
CN –Wild Thyme
T –P
CR –P/Sun/Dry
MH–3
C –Crimson
BP –S
S/L –3,580,000
MG–50

SN –Viola cornuta
CN –Johnny Jump-up
T –P
CR –P/Sun/Moist
MH–6
C –Purple/Yellow/Blue
BP –S/F
S/L –640,000
MG–55

GLOSSARY

Adjacent Vegetation. The existing vegetation next to a community of plant material that may influence its growth and development.

Alee. Downwind side of a mountain.

Algae. Primitive aquatic plants that lack stems or roots.

Alpine. Growing in mountain regions above the timberline.

Annual. A plant that completes its life cycle in one year.

Aquatic Plants. Plants that live in or near water.

Association. A plant community of definite composition.

Baffle. A plant form used to control the view in a wild garden.

Bark. The outermost tissue of a tree.

Barrier. A plant form used to control traffic in a wild garden.

Blending. The mixing of different plant species.

Boreal. Northern region of plant geographic distribution.

Canopy Layer. The highest layer of plants in the forest garden (also called the overstory).

Climax vegetation. The final stage of vegetative growth in a plant community.

Coniferous. Cone-bearing.

Crown. The upper portion of a plant.

Deciduous. Sheds foliage at the end of a growing season.

Dormancy. Temporarily inactive period in a plant's life cycle (as during winter or a drought).

Ecology. The relationship of plants to their surroundings.

Ecosystem. A community of plants considered together as a unit.

Endangered species. Those plants (and animals) in danger of becoming extinct.

Evergreen. A plant that retains its leaves throughout the year.

Floodplain. The area bordering a river or stream.

Foliage. The leaves of a plant.

Forb. An herbaceous plant other than grass.

Grassland. A region where grasses are the dominant plant materials.

Growth rate. The increase in size of a plant from year to year.

Habitat. The specialized environment where a plant lives.

Hardy plants. Those plants that can withstand the conditions of a rough climate or well-trafficked garden.

Herb. A seed-bearing nonwoody plant material.

Human impact. The effect of human intrusion on plant life.

Humus. A dark organic substance found in soil.

Inorganic. Mineral.

Invader species. The initial vegetation stage of successional growth.

Lichen. Crustlike plants that grow on rocks and trees.

Maturity. The last phase of plant growth.

Montane. Growing in mountain regions below the timberline.

Native. Naturally growing in a given geographic area.

Niche. The specific place within an ecosystem where a given species survives to its best advantage.

Nutrient. Food for plants.

Ornamental. A plant cultivated specifically for its beauty.

Overstory tree. A tree that forms part of the canopy (the highest layer of plant life in a forest).

pH. The measure of acidity/alkalinity.

Perennial. A plant that lives as long as the habitat remains favorable.

Plant form. The shape and structure of a plant.

Prairie. Large area of rolling grassland with fertile soil and very few trees.

Season. The period of time during which plants bloom or carry out another specific stage in their growth cycle.

Succession. The natural evolution of an ecosystem over time.

Tolerant. Capable of withstanding a given climatic or other environmental condition.

Understory. The seedling or larger trees that grow beneath larger (overstory) tree species.

Zone. An area of plant growth determined by specific environmental conditions.

INDEX

PICTURE CREDITS

Courtesy of Applewood Seed Co.: p. 20(b)

Karen Bussolini: p. 17(l)

Manuel DosPassos: p. 46(tr), p. 71

Sandra DosPassos: p. 24 (t), p. 26, p. 36(t), p. 41(l)

Courtesy of Environmental Seed Producers: p. 33, p. 56(l)

Derek Fell: p. 6(all), p. 7(all), p. 11, p. 12, p. 13(tr,br), p. 14(all), p. 16(all), p. 17(top), p. 19(all), p. 23, p. 21(all), p. 24(b,l), p. 25(tl,tr), p. 27(all), p. 28(l), p. 29(l), p. 30(all), p. 31(all), p. 32, p. 34(l), p. 35(r), p. 36(b), p. 37(all), p. 38(t,c), p. 39, p. 40, p. 44, p. 45(all), p. 51(l,br), p. 52, p. 54, p. 55(all), p. 57, p. 61, p. 62(all), p. 64(all), p. 66(all), p. 67(l), p. 68, p. 69(tl,bl)

Keith Glasgow: p. 13(l), p. 17(r), p. 25(b), p. 34(r), p. 35(l), p. 38(b), p. 51(tr), p. 67(br), p. 69(tr,br)

Richard Lindner: p. 28(r), p. 29(r)

Jonathan Pite: p. 34(c)

Josephine Zeitlin: p. 20(t), p. 24(br), p. 29(c), p. 41(r), p. 47(tl), p. 49(r), p. 56(r), p. 67(tr)

KEY TO ILLUSTRATION CODES:
tl: top left; tr: top right; bl: bottom left; br: bottom right; t: top; b: bottom; l: left; r: right; c: center